WICKED COOL PHP

WICKED COOL PHP

Real-World Scripts That Solve Difficult Problems

by William Steinmetz
with Brian Ward

no starch
press

San Francisco

12 11 10 09   4 5 6 7 8 9

ISBN-10: 1-59327-173-5
ISBN-13: 978-1-59327-173-2

Publisher: William Pollock
Production Editor: Megan Dunchak
Cover and Interior Design: Octopod Studios
Developmental Editor: Tyler Ortman
Technical Reviewer: Scott Gilbertson
Copyeditor: Linda Recktenwald
Compositor: Riley Hoffman
Proofreader: Jeanne Hansen
Indexer: Karin Arrigoni

For information on book distributors or translations, please contact No Starch Press, Inc. directly:

No Starch Press, Inc.
555 De Haro Street, Suite 250, San Francisco, CA 94107
phone: 415.863.9900; fax: 415.863.9950; info@nostarch.com; www.nostarch.com

Library of Congress Cataloging-in-Publication Data

Steinmetz, William.
  Wicked cool PHP : real-world scripts that solve difficult problems / William Steinmetz and Brian Ward. --
1st ed.
       p. cm.
  Includes index.
  ISBN-13: 978-1-59327-173-2
  ISBN-10: 1-59327-173-5
 1. PHP (Computer program language) I. Ward, Brian, 1972- II. Title.
QA76.73.P224S74 2008
005.13'3--dc22
                                        2005033702

BRIEF CONTENTS

CONTENTS IN DETAIL

3
PHP SECURITY 33

4
WORKING WITH FORMS 45

5
WORKING WITH TEXT AND HTML 59

8
USER AND SESSION TRACKING 103

9
WORKING WITH EMAIL 119

10
WORKING WITH IMAGES 129

11
USING cURL TO INTERACT WITH WEB SERVICES 141

12
INTERMEDIATE PROJECTS

155

INTRODUCTION

This book is for the developer who has stumbled on to PHP and wants to know how to get things done. You should know the basics of programming, and chances are you've seen many online code samples. But you may be wondering why some examples are much more complicated than others when they do the same thing.

Care has been taken to keep the examples in this book as simple as possible and to explain as much as possible about every piece of code. To keep client and server code confusion to a minimum, there isn't much JavaScript here. Everyone's impatient, so Chapter 1, "The FAQs of Life—The Scripts Every PHP Programmer Wants (or Needs) to Know," contains quick solutions to everyone's favorite little tasks and problems. After you calm down, take a look at Chapter 2, "Configuring PHP," to find out how you should install and configure PHP—quite a large number of problems arise from misconfiguration. Continuing in this vein, Chapter 3, "PHP Security," deals with keeping your scripts secure.

Chapter 4, "Working with Forms," returns to basics—specifically, how to get user input from forms and other dynamic input sources. Chapter 5, "Working with Text and HTML," shows how to process text and strings with a number of tools, including regular expressions. Chapter 6, "Working with Dates," discusses how to work with times and dates in PHP and MySQL, and Chapter 7, "Working with Files," deals with file manipulation.

With these fundamentals covered, Chapter 8, "User and Session Tracking," covers the details of session tracking and management. With multiple users on a complex website, it's important to keep track of what each user is doing so that one user's session doesn't interfere with another's.

Chapter 9, "Working with Email," and Chapter 10, "Working with Images," cover email and image manipulation, respectively. These tasks are often ill-suited for webserver scripts, so the chapters describe relatively lightweight tasks that can add significant value to your site.

In Chapter 11, "Using cURL to Interact with Web Services," you'll learn how to make your server interact with web services on other sites via XML.

Finally, Chapter 12, "Intermediate Projects," contains three fun little projects that can be incorporated into larger websites. These projects build on what you've learned elsewhere in the book.

1

THE FAQs OF LIFE—THE SCRIPTS EVERY PHP PROGRAMMER WANTS (OR NEEDS) TO KNOW

The scripts contained in this chapter answer several questions that clog PHP forums and discussion groups all over the world. They include the following:

- How do I add Previous/Next links to my shopping cart?
- Is there an easy way to make every other row in my table a different color?
- I have a big array that I need to sort—help!
- What's the best templating system to make the same HTML enclose my data on every page?

Although there are more complicated scripts later in this book, and many others that you may find more valuable, these scripts answer the questions that I see again and again. The only thing these beginning scripts have in common is that they're either the things that everyone *should* know or the things that everyone *wants* to know. Hand this chapter to a beginning PHP programmer you love. She'll thank you for it.

NOTE   *If you're not afraid to start rooting around on your webserver, Chapter 2 will also help the beginning PHP scripter and can make life a lot easier for the midlevel PHP programmer. You might want to go there next.*

#1: Including Another File as a Part of Your Script

Most serious applications have a core library of variables and scripts that are used on almost every page. For example, if you're writing a shopping cart that connects to a MySQL database, you could declare the MySQL login name and password on each page of your cart. But what if you need to change the password? Changing and uploading every file in your shopping cart could become a huge issue.

Rather than declaring the password in each of your page scripts, you can store that name and password in a separate file. You can then include that file as a part of your script, and whatever variables you declare in that file will be declared in your script!

Furthermore, you can store long scripts or functions in a separate file and include them only when you need them. For example, the function that gets real-time UPS shipping quotes is 24KB worth of XML processing goodness, but you use it only when someone chooses UPS as a shipping option. Why not store it in ups_ship_quotes.php and call it only when necessary?

In fact, almost all heavy-duty PHP applications have a file called something like config.php, which declares the critical variables that every page needs to know, such as the MySQL name and password. Those same applications also store frequently used scripts in different directories. Programmers then mix and match, taking the check-to-see-if-a-user-is-logged-in script from one directory, including the get-the-relevant-data-from-the-database script from another directory, and writing a central script that screens the data based on whether the user is logged in or not.

And here's how to do it.

```php
<?php

require_once("/path/to/file.php");

?>
```

The file that you give to require_once() is now a part of your script, exactly as if you had cut and copied the contents of the file into your script. You can even include HTML files to create a crude templating system.

No matter what you name the file, PHP tries to read it as if it were valid PHP. As with any PHP file, you need the <?php and ?> markers around the PHP code in your included file; otherwise, PHP simply prints the entire file (even if it's a binary).

You can use require_once() just like any other statement, so feel free to embed it into control structures.

```
if ($we_need_this_file === true) {
    require_once("needed_file.php");
}
```

What Can Go Wrong?

Several things can go awry when you're including a file.

The path to the script is wrong.
If this happens, the script returns a fatal error and dies. If you'd like to ensure that the script will run even if it can't find an include file, use include_once() instead of require_once().

The path to the script is correct, but the script is in a forbidden directory.
This can happen if you've configured the open_basedir setting to restrict the directories that PHP can access. Web developers restrict access to important files and directories for security purposes. We'll show you how to change directory permissions in "#16: Restricting the Files that PHP Can Access " on page 26.

The include file has a blank line or space before or after the code in the PHP script.
If your script sets cookies or does anything else to create a nonstandard HTTP, it must do so *before* sending any output to the browser. Remember, PHP prints anything outside of its <?php and ?> markers in an include file. Therefore, if you have a blank line before or after these markers, that line will be sent to the browser just as if it was plain HTML, and once HTML is sent to the browser, cookies cannot be set and sessions cannot be started. If you're including a script, make sure it has no whitespace outside the PHP tags. Be especially careful of spaces after the ?> end marker, because you normally can't see them when editing.

NOTE *Cookies are used for tracking users and storing hidden information. See Chapter 8 for more details.*

The include file can be viewed by non-PHP methods.
You can store PHP variables in any file regardless of its filename, but if you don't specifically configure Apache to make those files unreadable, Apache can serve them up as plaintext to anyone who asks. Therefore, anyone who knows the names of your include files can read *everything in them* if you're not careful.

Needless to say, storing your MySQL passwords and master account names in a place where anyone with Internet Explorer can see them is *not* considered good security practice.

To tighten security, you can place include files outside the web directories (preferably in a password-protected directory) so people can access the script only through FTP. In fact, if you're dealing with sensitive information such as credit card authorization data, you should feel obligated to do so.

NOTE *We'll see how to validate a credit card number in "#30: Validating a Credit Card" on page 52.*

You're in include overload.

I once purchased a shopping cart program because it was written in PHP, and I planned to customize the scripts to fit my business. Imagine my surprise when I found out that the central module of the cart's script (where people added, deleted, and adjusted items) consisted of 7 includes, 12 lines of actual code, and 3 Smarty templates. I opened one of the included files, and it was—you guessed it—a series of three additional includes.

Includes can make your code very compact. But take it from me: If you're trying to decipher how a hyper-included script works, it's a *living hell.* For the sake of other programmers and future generations, *please don't include a file without a comment that tells people what that included file does.* Thank you.

You're using unchecked variables as include filenames.

Although you *can* do something like include($file) to open the correct script depending on what a user chooses, doing so may allow a hacker to include any file in the site with a bit of tweaking or, depending on your server settings, a file on *his* site, which then breaks into your server. In fact, a couple of PHP-based worms rely on badly written scripts like this. Moreover, these types of scripts are far more prone to strange bugs and are generally impossible to read.

If you must include a range of files with a variable, use a script like the one shown in "#28: Making Sure a Response Is One of a Set of Given Values" on page 51 to verify that the filenames are permissible, which prevents someone from opening your root password file.

#2: Highlighting Alternate Row Colors in a Table

When you have lots of information presented in rows, such as topics in a forum or line items in a shopping cart, individual rows are much easier to read when every other row is a slightly different color. The first step is to define colors for table rows in your style sheet.

```
tr.row1 {
    background-color: gray;
}

tr.row2 {
    background-color: white;
}
```

There are two style classes here for table row tags (`<tr>`), row1 and row2. As with any CSS, you can place this inside a preexisting CSS file that your document includes or enclose it within `<style>` `</style>` tags in your document head.

Now let's define a function that alternately returns these classes. There's a little trick here—you pass an integer variable to this function by reference. The function automatically updates this variable so that you can make repeated calls without worrying about the current state of the table:

```
function table_row_format(&$row_counter) {
    // Returns row class for a row
    if ($row_counter & 1) {
        $row_color = "row2";
    } else {
        $row_color = "row1";
    }
    $row_counter++;
    return $row_color;
}
```

Now let's see how to use this function. First, let's set up an SQL query to some rows of data from the table described in the appendix and start the table formatting:

```
$sql = "SELECT product_name FROM product_info";
$result = @mysql_query($sql, $db) or die;

echo "<table>";
```

The rest is easy; we just need to initialize the row state variable (here, `$i`), repeatedly call `table_row_format($i)` to get the alternating row style classes, and then give each row the correct class attribute. Finally, we close the table:

```
$i = 0;
while($row = mysql_fetch_array($result)) {
    /* Print results. */
    $row_class = table_row_format($i);
    echo "<tr class=\"$row_class\"><td>$row[product_name]</td></tr>";
}
echo "</table>";
```

The key to using the `table_row_format()` function is understanding how it works. You always initialize an integer variable for the state, but it doesn't matter what the value is, because `table_row_format()` takes care of it for you.

Hacking the Script

There are a million cheap tricks you can do with the style sheet. For more details on CSS, consult the online resource of your choice, or take a look at *Cascading Style Sheets: The Definitive Guide, 2nd Edition,* by Eric Meyer (O'Reilly

Media, 2004). Perhaps more interestingly, you can easily convert this function into an object-oriented table formatter. Instead of explicitly declaring a state variable, you can make a class with a private variable to keep track of the state. The constructor and destructor open and close the table tags, respectively. Here's what the class looks like:

```
class AltTable {
    function __construct() {
        $this->state = 0;
        print "<table>";
    }
    function __destruct() {
        print "</table>";
    }
    function print_row($row) {
        if ($this->state & 1) {
            $row_color = "row2";
        } else {
            $row_color = "row1";
        }
        print "<tr class=\"$row_color\">";
        foreach ($row as $value) {
            print "<td>$value</td>";
        }
        print "</tr>";
        $this->state++;
    }
}
```

And here's how to use the class (assume that the query is the same as the preceding example):

```
$mytable = new AltTable;
while($row = mysql_fetch_row($result)) {
    /* Print results. */
    $mytable->print_row($row);
}
unset($mytable);
```

At first glance, you may think that this is great because it's a little easier to use—you don't have to mess with a state variable, the print_row() method can handle any number of columns, and you don't even have to write any HTML to start and finish the table. This is certainly a great advantage if all your tables look the same. However, this tidiness is at the cost of flexibility and some efficiency. Sure, you can add methods and attributes to do some fancy stuff such as add table headers, but you need to ask yourself if it's really worth it.

#3: Creating Previous/Next Links

If you need to display a large number of items on a page, you may want to simplify the display by breaking it into several pages with a limited number of items per page. By doing so, you make your results easier to view and speed page-loading times.

A navigation bar gives the users control of these pages. You want a bar with Previous and Next links, as well as direct page number links. Here's a script that does it all:

```php
<?php
function create_navbar($start_number = 0, $items_per_page = 50, $count) {
    // Creates a navigation bar
    $current_page = $_SERVER["PHP_SELF"];

    if (($start_number < 0) || (! is_numeric($start_number))) {
        $start_number = 0;
    }

    $navbar = "";
    $prev_navbar = "";
    $next_navbar = "";

    if ($count > $items_per_page) {
        $nav_count = 0;
        $page_count  = 1;
        $nav_passed = false;

        while ($nav_count < $count) {
            // Are we at the current page position?
            if (($start_number <= $nav_count) && ($nav_passed != true)) {
                $navbar .= "<b><a href=\"$current_page?start=$nav_count\">
[$page_count] </a></b>";
                $nav_passed = true;
                // Do we need a "prev" button?
                if ($start_number != 0) {
                    $prevnumber = $nav_count - $items_per_page;
                    if ($prevnumber < 1) {
                        $prevnumber = 0;
                    }
                    $prev_navbar = "<a href=\"$current_page?start=$prevnumber\
"> &lt;&lt;Prev - </a>";
                }

                $nextnumber = $items_per_page + $nav_count;

                // Do we need a "next" button?
                if ($nextnumber < $count) {
```

```
                              $next_navbar = "<a href=\"
$current_page?start=$nextnumber\"> - Next&gt;&gt; </a><br>";
                   }
         } else {
             // Print normally.
               $navbar .= "<a href=\"$current_page?start=$nav_count\">
[$page_count] </a>";
         }

         $nav_count += $items_per_page;
         $page_count++;
      }

      $navbar = $prev_navbar . $navbar . $next_navbar;
      return $navbar;
   }
}


?>
```

Let's assume you're going to use this script to process information that you're retrieving from a database. Two things will make the display accurate and efficient:

Show only a subset of rows from your database.

If the idea is to show only 25 items per page, then you should write a SQL query that returns only 25 items. (Okay, you *could* select everything and then loop through the entire result set, sifting through thousands of rows until you find the 25 you want, but there is a better way.) Furthermore, you want to show a *specific* 25 items. Pulling the first 25 items from the database isn't helpful when the user wants to look at products #176 through #200.

Fortunately, both objectives are easily accomplished with the SQL LIMIT clause, which retrieves only a set number of rows from a database. Your SQL query should look something like this:

```
SELECT * FROM your_table
WHERE conditions
LIMIT $start_number, $items_per_page
```

When added to the end of a query, the LIMIT clause pulls only a selected number of rows from the result set. For example, placing `LIMIT 75, 25` at the end of a query retrieves 25 rows from the database, starting at the 75th row.

NOTE *If you use a number for the starting row that's greater than the number of rows, MySQL returns no data. For example, if you run `LIMIT 200, 25` and there are only 199 rows in your table, you get an empty result set instead of an error. Well-written programs account for empty sets by using an `if (mysql_num_rows($result) > 0)` check.*

Now that you have only the rows that you want, you still need to do one other thing.

Count the total number of rows in your result set.

Result set is a fancy SQL way of saying "whatever data is returned after all the where statements are processed." We need the total count to know what page we're currently on and how many more pages we have to go until we've finished. Without the total count, we might display a Next link when there are no more items to see, and we wouldn't be able to tell the user how many more pages there are to look at.

Your SQL query should look like this:

```
SELECT count(*) AS count FROM your_table
WHERE conditions
```

Once you've gotten this valuable information, you then plug three pieces of information into the create_navbar() function. The create_navbar() function contains several variables, so let's look at each of them:

$current_page The current page that contains the navigation bar. In this script, we use the $_SERVER["PHP_SELF"] special variable, which is always set to the current page without the hostname and any GET parameters. For example, in a script accessed at http://example.com/navbar.php?start=0, $current_page would be set to /navbar.php.

$start_number The starting row number. For example, if the user is looking at rows 100 through 125, the start number is 100. This number is passed on via the GET method in the URL as the startnum parameter. The default is 0.

$items_per_page The number of rows users see on each page. For example, if you have 100 rows of data, an $items_per_page value of 25 results in four pages with 25 rows each. The same 100 rows with an $items_per_page value of 50 produces a scant two pages. And if the $items_per_page value is 200, a set of 100 rows has no navigation bar, because everything fits in a single page. This script's default $items_per_page value is 50.

$count The total number of data rows. I showed you how to get this information in "Count the total number of rows in your result set" above.

$nav_count This variable starts at 0 and keeps incrementing by $items_per_page until it is greater than $count. When the value exceeds $count, the script has reached the end of result set—and thus the end of the navigation bar.

$page_count The number of pages in the result set.

$nav_passed A temporary variable that is set to Y the first time $nav_count exceeds $start_number; in other words, when we're looking at the current page. This allows us to highlight the current page number in the navigation bar display.

Using the Script

```php
<?php

$start_number = intval($_GET["start"]);
$items_per_page = 100;
$category_sales = null;

if ($start_number >= 0) {

    // Count the items in the category.
    $sql = "SELECT count(*) AS count FROM product_info
            WHERE category = 'shoes'";
    $result = @mysql_query($sql, $connect_string) or die("Error is  " .
mysql_error());
    while($row = mysql_fetch_array($result)) {
        $count = $row['count'];
    }

    // Now get the results to show to the customer.
    $sql = "SELECT product_id, product_name FROM product_info
            WHERE category = 'shoes'
            LIMIT $start_number, $items_per_page";
    $result = @mysql_query($sql, $connect_string) or die("Error is  " .
mysql_error());
    if (mysql_num_rows($result) > 0) {
        while($row = mysql_fetch_array($result)) {
            // Loop through and add your HTML display info
            // into $category_sales.
            $category_sales .= "Data from SQL query";
        }
    } else {
        $category_sales = "There were no items in this category.";
    }

    $navbar = create_navbar($start_number, $items_per_page, $count);
}

if (is_null($category_sales)) {
    echo "Invalid input.";
} else {
    echo "$navbar<br />$category_sales";
}

?>
```

This example shows how to use the create_navbar() function in conjunction with a set of data from a database table (see the appendix for the data details). The script works as follows:

1. The starting row number is extracted from a GET parameter into the $start_number variable.

2. An initial SQL query extracts the total number of displayable rows in the table.

3. A second query extracts at most $items_per_page rows from the table, starting at $start_number.

4. The row data is formatted.

5. The create_navbar() function creates the navigation bar; the formatted bar goes in the $navbar variable.

6. The script prints the formatted navigation bar and data.

#4: Printing the Contents of an Array

Let's say that you have been adding and subtracting items from an array, but you're running into some problems. What you really need is to view the contents of an array as they were at a specific line in your script. There's a really easy way to do this that doesn't get *nearly* the attention that it should from PHP tutorials around the world—the print_r() function! Here's an example:

```php
<?php

$alacarte = array("chocolate ice cream",
                  "vanilla pudding",
                  "snozzberry whip");
$menu = array ("appetizer" => "fruit",
               "entree" => "roast beef",
               "dessert" => $alacarte);

print_r($menu);

?>
```

The print_r() function prints arrays onscreen in a format that humans can read. This is especially handy when you're dealing with *multidimensional arrays* (which, if you're not familiar with the term, are arrays that contain other arrays). Feed an array to print_r(), and you get a simple plaintext display. Because it uses whitespace but no HTML markup, you may need to view the page source to see it as it is meant to be seen. The previous sample results in this output:

```
Array
(
    [appetizer] => fruit
    [entree] => roast beef
    [dessert] => Array
        (
            [0] => chocolate ice cream
            [1] => vanilla pudding
            [2] => snozzberry whip
        )

)
```

#5: Turning an Array into a Nonarray Variable That Can Be Restored Later

Although arrays are tremendously useful, there are some places where they're just not welcome. You can't directly store an array inside a cookie or a session, for instance. MySQL and XML can't handle the native PHP array type, either.

Fortunately, there's a way to transform PHP arrays into strings that you can store nearly anywhere: the serialize() function. Here's a script that illustrates how this function works (assume $alacarte is the same as it was in the preceding section):

```php
<?php

$menu = array(
    "appetizer" => "fruit",
    "entree" => "roast beef",
    "dessert" => $alacarte);

$menu_s = serialize($menu);

echo $menu_s;

?>
```

Running this script produces the following output:

```
PEa:3:{s:9:"appetizer";s:5:"fruit";s:6:"entree";s:10:"roast
beef";s:7:"dessert";a:3:{i:0;s:19:"chocolate ice cream";i:1;s:15:"vanilla
pudding";i:2;s:15:"snozzberry whip";}}
```

You can store this value nearly anywhere—in cookies, databases, hidden POST input fields, and so on. When you need to restore the serialized array to a real array, use unserialize(), as follows:

```php
$menu = unserialize($menu_s);
```

What Can Go Wrong?

serialize() is a wonderful function, but there are a couple of things you should know. First, people can read serialized arrays fairly easily, so if you're storing sensitive arrays in cookies or sessions, you probably want to encrypt them first so that intruders can't sniff your data. (See "#23: Encrypting Data with Mcrypt" on page 41.)

Don't abuse this function. If you find yourself consistently storing arrays in databases, or if you start getting serialized strings, you should probably redesign your database structure or storage mechanism.

Finally, you should avoid passing serialized arrays along with the HTTP GET method, because URLs have a fairly short finite length.

#6: Sorting Multidimensional Arrays

One perennial programming task is to sort complicated arrays. For example, let's say that you have this array:

```
$items = array(
    array("name" => "Mojo Nixon", "price" => 19.96, "quantity" => 2),
    array("name" => "ABBA", "price" => 14.99, "quantity" => 1),
    array("name" => "Iced Earth", "price" => 12.96, "quantity" => 4),
);
```

Your goal is to sort this by the name key in each subarray. PHP, like many other scripting languages, has a sort function named usort() that sorts by a user-defined comparison function. In other words, you can sort an array by any criteria you like, and you don't need to fuss with the mechanics of sorting algorithms. The name-based sorting script with usort() boils down to this:

```
function name_cmp($a, $b) {
    return strcasecmp($a["name"], $b["name"]);
}

usort($items, "name_cmp");
```

If this script looks simple, that's because it is. The user-defined comparison function is called name_cmp. usort() and uses the comparison function to compare two elements. Those elements are the arguments (here, $a and $b). All you need to do in your comparison function is figure out how $a relates to $b:

- If $a is less than $b, it should return -1.
- If $a is equal to $b, it should return 0.
- If $a is greater than $b, it should return 1.

Because $a and $b are arrays in our comparison function, and we're interested in the values under the name keys in these arrays, we want to compare $a["name"] and $b["name"]. This is easy enough to do with a bunch of if/then statements, but because these are strings, you should use the strcasecmp() built-in function for speed, clarity, and bug avoidance.

NOTE *There's a PHP function called array_multisort() that attempts to be a catchall solution for multidimensional array sorting. It's ruthlessly complicated; you're probably better off avoiding it.*

Hacking the Script

The most obvious modification you can make to the comparison function is to add extra criteria in case two elements are equal. Using our previous example, here's how to sort by price in case the names are the same:

```
function name_cmp($a, $b) {
    $r = strcasecmp($a["name"], $b["name"]);
    if ($r == 0) {
        if ($a["price"] < $b["price"]) {
            $r = -1;
        } elseif ($a["price"] > $b["price"]) {
            $r = 1;
        } else {
            $r = 0;
            /* Not strictly necessary; $r is already 0. */
        }
    }
    return($r);
}
```

#7: Templating Your Site with Smarty

Most sites have a consistent look and feel. Although the dynamic content in the middle of the page may change, there's usually a header, a navigation bar on the side, and maybe an advertisement or two. There are simple ways to achieve this, from custom header-printing functions to include files. Depending on the size of your site, these solutions may work fine, but the larger and more complicated your content becomes, the more tedious making changes can get.

The most common templating solution is Smarty (http://smarty.php .net/). With Smarty, you create templates with variables. In other words, you can create one HTML file with placeholders for PHP-created data. In addition, you can include other Smarty templates inside a template, allowing you to better organize and edit pieces of your site. Once you get *really* familiar with Smarty, you can cache data and speed up your site considerably, but that's an advanced technique outside the scope of this book.

What follows is enough to get you up and running for most sites.

Installing Smarty

Follow these steps to install Smarty on your server.

1. Create a directory on your server within the web root named *smarty* to store the core Smarty files.

2. Go to http://smarty.php.net/ and download the latest version of Smarty. Decompress and extract it to a folder on your computer.

3. Transfer all Smarty files from your computer to the smarty directory on your server.

4. On your server, create another directory called *templates* for your Smarty templates. Create two subdirectories here: *html* for the raw templates and *compile* for Smarty-compiled templates.

5. Make the compile directory writeable by the webserver. If you're not sure how to do that, "File Permissions" on page 91 will show you the way.

6. In the templates directory, create (or upload) a file called smarty_initialize.php, containing the following:

```php
<?php

define ("SMARTY_DIR", "/path/to/web/root/smarty/");

require_once (SMARTY_DIR."Smarty.class.php");
$smarty = new Smarty;
$smarty->compile_dir = "/path/to/web/root/templates/compile";
$smarty->template_dir = "/path/to/web/root/templates/html";

?>
```

Four aspects of the smarty_initialize.php file are very important:

- The `SMARTY_DIR` constant points at the Smarty library directory.
- To load the library, smarty_initialize.php requires the Smarty.class.php file.
- Because Smarty is object-oriented, you must create a new Smarty object. This script does so with `$smarty = new Smarty`.
- Smarty needs to know where your template and compile directories are. Two object attributes (`compile_dir` and `template_dir`) control this location.

Now that you've got Smarty set up, it's time to learn how to use it.

A Brief Smarty Tutorial

Let's look at the Smarty language. In the smarty_initialize.php file outlined in the previous section, Smarty templates go in the templates/html directory. Typically, template files are everyday HTML, JavaScript, CSS, or anything else that you'd want to send to a web browser. Let's say that you have some HTML in a template named basic.tpl. To make Smarty display this template, use Smarty's `display()` method, as shown in the following code:

```php
<?php
require_once("smarty_initialize.php");
$smarty->display("basic.tpl");
?>
```

To access the true power of Smarty, you need to put PHP-created data into a template. Use curly braces with a dollar sign ($) to create a Smarty variable. To show you how it works, we'll assume that our basic.tpl file looks like this:

```
<HTML>
<head>
<title>{$assigned_title}</title>
</head>
<body>
My name is {$assigned_name}.
</body>
```

There are two variables here, $assigned_title and $assigned_name. To set the variables so that Smarty displays those values, use the assign() method, as follows:

```
<?php

require_once("smarty_initialize.php");

$page_title = "The Smarty Template Test";
$page_name = "William Steinmetz";

$smarty->assign("assigned_title", $page_title);
$smarty->assign("assigned_name", $page_name);

$smarty->display("basic.tpl");

?>
```

You can assign the variable to just about any kind of PHP string data; it doesn't matter if it's MySQL data, HTML from some other source, user-supplied data, or what have you. If everything goes smoothly, the HTML renders as shown in Figure 1-1.

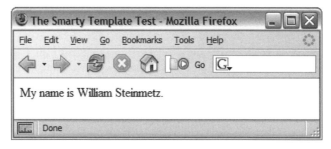

Figure 1-1: HTML displayed in a browser

What Can Go Wrong?

Aside from typical mundane incorrect path errors, the most common error that you'll encounter is that the webserver cannot write to the compile directory you've defined for the compiled Smarty templates. If the compile directory does not have *write* and *execute* permissions for the server, Smarty attempts to write the new files, fails, and chokes. The page still displays, but instead of your template, an ugly warning comes back.

You should also make sure that you assign all of your variables. If you don't assign one with the $smarty->assign() function, Smarty uses an empty string as a default. This won't cause a Smarty error, but your page looks very ugly, and some elements may not work the way you intended.

Hacking the Script

You should be aware of a couple of additional things in order to make the best use of Smarty's power. For example, you can include multiple templates in a script, as follows:

```php
<?php

// Initialize the Smarty file.
require_once("smarty_initialize.php");

// Display the first Smarty template.
$smarty->display("header.tpl");

echo "Middle stuff<br />";

// Display the second Smarty template.
$smarty->display("footer.tpl");

?>
```

There are times when you have complicated templates composed of several pieces. For example, if you have a banner ad inside a header.tpl file that seldom changes, you may want the flexibility of being able to edit the ad in a separate file. You can tell Smarty to display an advertisement.tpl file within the header.tpl file like this:

```
<tr><td><img src="logo.gif"></td>
<td>
{include file="advertisement.tpl"}
</td>
</tr>
```

Smarty is very powerful—for example, you can construct tables in such a way that you can format an entire table just by assigning a PHP array to a Smarty variable. There are rudimentary if/then functions, caching abilities, prefiltering and postfiltering functions, and more. Now that you know how Smarty works, it's a good idea to check out the online documentation for more uses.

2

CONFIGURING PHP

As with any software package, PHP has many configuration options that affect how it runs. Most of those options aren't significant, but there are a few important ones that every programmer should know.

In addition, there are many add-ons for PHP, called *libraries*, that add new capabilities to PHP. For example, the cURL extension allows your server to send form data to other servers and process the data that gets sent back. Mcrypt, another useful extension, allows you to easily perform high-end encryption so you can store sensitive data securely.

This chapter shows you the settings that programmers frequently use in PHP and when you'd want to use them.

Configuration Settings and the php.ini File

Most novice programmers treat PHP's default settings as if they were a tenant moving into an apartment complex—afraid to make changes lest it cost them their security deposit. But you should really think of PHP as your house. You're going to live here for a while, so why not rearrange the furniture and knock down a wall or two?

NOTE   *Depending on your webserver host, you may not be able to change the settings yourself. However, good hosting services should be willing to make the change for you, and many high-end server hosts allow you to alter directives with a user-specific configuration file.*

PHP's settings are in a file called php.ini that you can view and change with any text editor. The settings are arranged into sections and look something like this:

```
max_execution_time = 30    ; Maximum execution time
max_input_time = 60        ; Maximum input parsing time
memory_limit = 8M          ; Maximum memory a script may consume
```

You can set configuration parameters with an equal sign (=). A semicolon (;) denotes a comment; however, there are a few exceptions with semicolons in some parameters. If you'd like to change a setting permanently, make a backup of your php.ini, edit the original, and restart Apache. If you'd rather change it on a per-script basis, use the ini_set() function.

Locating Your php.ini File

Sometimes it can be a little difficult to track down the location of php.ini on your system, especially if there are multiple instances of a PHP installation. Here are a few ways of finding it:

- On Unix systems, look in /usr/lib or /usr/local/lib. It should be in the lib directory of wherever you installed PHP.
- On Windows, try C:\Program Files\PHP.
- Call the phpinfo() function in a PHP script (see the following section for more detail). The location appears in the output near the beginning with the label *Configuration File (php.ini) Location*.
- On many Unix systems, the locate php.ini command returns all filenames that match php.ini.

NOTE   *Many settings aren't in the default php.ini file; PHP uses defaults for the values not specified. A listing of the default settings for PHP can be found at http://www.php.net/manual/en/ini.php.*

#8: Revealing All of PHP's Settings

PHP has many features, but not all may be enabled or built in your installation. If you want to see what your particular PHP installation has, a very simple script can show you everything. However, the danger with this script is that it shows *so much* information that it practically hands a blueprint to potential crackers that says, "Here. These are the weak points. Please break into my system." Therefore, you should delete this script as soon as you're finished with it.

```php
<?php

phpinfo();

?>
```

The `phpinfo()` function prints everything that PHP knows about its configuration. I do mean *everything*. Not only does it show you the status of every single available PHP setting, the location of the php.ini file, and your PHP version, but it also tells you what version of webserver software you're running, what extensions are compiled with PHP, and what the server API is. It's very useful for looking at configuration options and to be certain you've properly installed and enabled a needed feature.

To run the script, visit the page with your web browser. Don't forget to delete it when finished.

#9: Reading an Individual Setting

Sometimes `phpinfo()` can be overkill if you know what you're looking for. For example, you may just want to find out whether magic quotes is turned on or check an include path. Furthermore, `phpinfo()` won't help you if you're writing a script that behaves one way if a setting is enabled and another way if it's not.

To get the value of a particular configuration setting, use the `ini_get()` function as follows:

```php
<?php
echo "The register_globals value is " . ini_get('register_globals');
?>
```

Give `ini_get()` a valid configuration parameter name, and it returns the current setting on the current server. The setting is returned as a regular value, so you can print it, assign it to a variable, and so on. However, there are two small things that you should be aware of.

First, Boolean values such as "false" are usually returned as a null string when you output them, so if register_globals is set to "off" you might see this output:

```
The register_globals value is
```

Second, numeric values are frequently stored in shorthand. For example, if the upload_max_filesize is set to 8,192 bytes, the value returned will be 8KB. Similarly, if the maximum size of an uploaded file is two megabytes, upload_max_filesize is not 2,097,152 bytes but rather 2MB.

This can be a problem if you need to do arithmetic operations on these numbers. The official PHP documentation includes this function that converts Ks and Ms to real numbers:

```php
function return_bytes($val) {
    $val = trim($val);
    $last = $val{strlen($val)-1};
    switch(strtoupper($last)) {
        case 'K':
            return (int) $val * 1024;
            break;
        case 'M':
            return (int) $val * 1048576;
            break;
        default:
            return $val;
    }
}
```

#10: Error Reporting

When you're writing code, it's very easy to forget about a variable name or to write deprecated code. At times, PHP is so user friendly (by programming standards) that it will actually work around many subtle coding mistakes.

For example, PHP allows you to write a program without declaring all of your variables at the start, which is convenient right up until you misspell $string as $stirng, and your program chokes on a null value. You can also pass variables to functions in totally incorrect ways that work *most* of the time because PHP makes some assumptions about what you meant. That's great until PHP guesses incorrectly, and then you'll be scratching your head over a mysterious bug.

To stop PHP from quietly fixing problems, you can enable *error reporting*, which will cause PHP to flood your screen with every problem—no matter how insignificant—that it finds. You can use these error messages to tighten potential security loopholes and catch bad variables before you go live with your program. To turn on error reporting, simply place the following code at the beginning of the script that you're writing:

```
<?php
error_reporting(E_ALL);
// The rest of your script goes here.
?>
```

Turning on error reporting causes PHP to print error messages to the screen before processing the rest of the program. (This makes it impossible to set cookies in the event of an error, so don't plan on changing cookie values the first time you turn on error reporting.)

Common Error Messages

The three most common error messages are worth understanding.

Notice: Undefined variable: *var* in *script.php* on line *n*

This message means that you are using a variable that you have not defined earlier in the script. This can happen in a variety of circumstances:

- You misspelled a variable name.

- You have a conditional that contains a variable definition, such as this:

```
if ($fred == "I'm Fred") {
    $he_is_fred = "yes";
}
```

- You're concatenating a variable without ever having explicitly declared it.

The next problem is one you're more likely to see in older PHP code that you're trying to use in your program:

Notice: Use of undefined constant k - assumed 'k' in *script.php* on line *n*

This warning message usually means that you're passing a string to a function without encapsulating it in quotes. In other words, you've used something like strtolower(*string*) instead of strtolower("*string*").

Finally, there is a common error message that you can get when accessing an array:

Notice: Undefined index: *i* in *script.php* on line *n*

In practical terms, this means that you tried to read $*array*[*i*], but $*array* was not defined at the index *i*. This error often pops up when you're getting a value from a form via $_POST or $_GET, but there was no value stored in either

$_POST or $_GET under that name. In practical terms, it usually means that the user didn't check the appropriate box or radio button (thus not giving it a value), or the variable wasn't passed on in the URL in a GET request.

You should disable this script error checking on your live site, because not only will users see it and bug you, but it will also interfere with cookies, meaning that you may have session-tracking problems.

#11: Suppressing All Error Messages

Sometimes you may have a script that works fine, but PHP still insists on kicking up a fuss. In other instances, if something should go wrong, you don't want your users to see an ugly error message (which reveals the sort of information hackers just love to see).

Fortunately, you can suppress all error messages through a setting in your php.ini file:

```
display_errors = Off
```

You should use this setting in your production environment so that you don't have to worry about the Internet at large seeing your PHP diagnostic messages. If you need to see these diagnostic messages to root out problems, use the following configuration setting to send the messages to the Apache log:

```
log_errors = On
```

If you like, you can even send the diagnostics to the syslog or a file by setting the error_log parameter to syslog or *filename*.

Your development environment is another story; there, you want as many diagnostic messages as you can stand. With the display_errors configuration setting on, you can set the error_reporting parameter in php.ini to a bitfield of your choosing (see the example php.ini file that comes with PHP for more details). However, if one script is being a particular pain in your development environment, and you just want it to shut up, use this function call in your script as a stopgap measure:

```
error_reporting(0);
```

#12: Extending the Run Time of a Script

At one point, the company I work for changed its online shopping carts, forcing me to write a script to convert 250MB of stored product data from the old cart's format into the new cart's format. The script worked perfectly, but I was evaluating and transforming so much data that PHP kept timing out my program after 30 seconds, long before it had a chance to finish.

That's when I discovered a configuration parameter that allowed me to get the job done. The following line, when added to the beginning of a script, allows the script to take up to 240 seconds to finish.

```
ini_set(max_execution_time, "240");
```

The `max_execution_time` configuration parameter controls the longest allowable time a script is allowed to run before it's automatically shut down. Be careful of abusing this parameter. If your script can't run in four minutes or less, you're either working on a much larger database than most people ever will, your script is terribly inefficient, or you're using the wrong programming language.

What Can Go Wrong?

Your server could be running in safe mode, which disables the run-time alteration of `max_execution_time`.

Also, double-check your code. Maybe you've got an infinite loop somewhere, or maybe you're running a loop inside a loop that does nothing.

#13: Preventing Users from Uploading Large Files

If you want to keep your users from uploading 70GB MPEGs of the latest *Star Wars* movie, you can set a maximum file size when users are uploading files to your server. (For information on how to process uploaded files, see "#54: Uploading Images to a Directory" on page 97.)

```
upload_max_filesize = 500K
```

You can specify the maximum file size in one of three ways:

- An integer (indicating the total number of bytes)
- Using a number and an M to indicate megabytes, as in *2M* (2 megabytes)
- Using a number and a K to indicate kilobytes, as in *8K* (8 kilobytes)

In any case, your users will now be unable to upload anything greater than the size you set. The default is 2MB.

#14: Turning Off Registered Global Variables

PHP has a legacy misfeature that makes it slightly easier to access GET and POST parameters. For example, if there is a POST parameter named `myparm`, PHP can automatically extract it and put it in a variable named `$myparm`. Unfortunately, this is a tremendous security risk, because you can set any global variable this way, and if you forget to initialize a variable, the user could manipulate vulnerable parts of your script.

You can disable this feature by turning the register_globals variable to Off in your server's php.ini file:

```
register_globals = Off
```

Fortunately, this feature is turned off on PHP versions 4.2 or higher. However, it's such a problem that you should always double-check.

#15: Enabling Magic Quotes

Magic Quotes is a handy utility used by server hosts to protect against SQL Injection Attacks (as shown in "#19: SQL Injection Attacks " on page 35). The idea is that whenever a form passes a variable to a PHP script, Magic Quotes automatically escapes all single quotes, double quotes, and back-slashes with a backslash, turning "Ferrett's Book" into \"Ferrett\'s Book\".

If you're using MySQL, this isn't an ideal solution—you should use the MySQL-tailored mysql_real_escape_string() function instead—but in a pinch, Magic Quotes will do. Here's how to enable it in your php.ini file:

```
magic_quotes_gpc = 1
```

What Can Go Wrong?

If you don't have Magic Quotes turned on, you'll have to use the mysql_real_escape_string() function to ensure that the data is escaped. However, if you use this function on form data when Magic Quotes is also enabled, you'll double the number of backslashes, turning \"Ferrett\'s Book\" into \\"Ferrett\\'s Book\\". As you can see, it pays to be consistent, because the strings in your database tables can accumulate backslashes if you're not careful.

#16: Restricting the Files that PHP Can Access

If you're worried about a malignant PHP script accessing system files (such as your password file), you can limit the directories that PHP has access to with the open_basedir setting. When open_basedir is enabled, PHP cannot open or otherwise manipulate any files outside of the defined directories. Here's a php.ini example that limits access to /home/www:

```
open_basedir = /home/www
```

You can add access to multiple directories by separating them with a colon (:) for Unix or a semicolon (;) in Windows.

NOTE *By default, PHP will allow access to the specified directory and all subdirectories below. If you'd like to limit this to only the files in the specified directory, add a slash to the end of the path; for example, /home/www/.*

What Can Go Wrong?

If your users need to upload files, a temporary file directory stores these files until you process them with your scripts. Because this directory is traditionally far away from the rest of the PHP files, you must remember to add it to the open_basedir access list.

#17: Shutting Down Specific Functions

Let's say that you have decided that the exec() function, which allows a PHP script to run commands directly on the server, is too dangerous. You can disable PHP functions individually, locking out the security risks while allowing the rest to run just fine. Here's an example of how to disable a number of functions in your php.ini file:

```
disable_functions = system, exec, passthru, shell_exec, proc_open
```

#18: Adding Extensions to PHP

If you're a serious developer, eventually you'll hit the limits of a stock PHP build. Although PHP has plenty of built-in capability, it does not have native encryption, graphics, a convenient way to access other web pages, or XML data access functions.

The way PHP accomplishes these tasks is through a number of *extensions* that employ third-party libraries to do the hard work. Some of the handier extensions are as follows.

cURL

cURL allows your PHP server to access other websites, sending and receiving information via a URL-like protocol. (You'll most commonly use HTTP, which lets you talk to other web pages, and FTP, which allows you to upload and download files.) In practical terms, this means you can have your server imitate a web browser, go to other sites, and download their web pages into a variable of your choosing.

cURL is a vital tool for any serious online shopping cart, because it allows you to approve credit card charges and get live shipping quotes for customers. You use cURL to connect and send transaction data to another company's server. The server replies, telling you information such as whether the charge was approved or denied and why.

Mcrypt

Ever need to encrypt something? Any sensitive information in cookies or sessions should be encrypted for security's sake, and if you're storing anything valuable like credit card numbers or other personal information, you *definitely* want to make sure that it can't be accessed via a raw database dump. Thankfully, the Mcrypt library allows you to perform high-level encryption without knowing anything about encryption techniques! (I'll show you how to use Mcrypt in "#23: Encrypting Data with Mcrypt" on page 41.)

GD

If you want to create graphics on demand or just get image information when you need it, GD is the library for you. GD allows you to work with JPEGs and GIF files, either creating them as you need them for things like charts, or altering them to create thumbnails of existing images.

MySQL

A completely vanilla build of PHP doesn't know how to access a database. Fortunately, since MySQL and PHP are like Zan and Jayna, most PHP-enabled webservers have the necessary MySQL libraries installed by default, so most people never know that the `mysql_connect()` function is part of an extension.

Other PHP extensions include SOAP (which allows you to access web services), PDF, and Verisign Payment Pro. It may seem like a great idea to add every extension in existence to PHP, but remember that each extension you add can slow initialization time and add security holes. Furthermore, extensions that aren't common often don't have someone actively maintaining them, leaving you without an upgrade path.

Adding PHP Extensions

Now that you know what's available through extensions, let's explore how to install them. The first step is to see if you already have what you're looking for.

Checking to See If Extensions Are Already Loaded

Many webservers have the more useful extensions installed by default, so before you go through the bother of installing an extension, first check to be certain you don't have it already installed and loaded.

The easiest way to check for extensions is run the `phpinfo()` function (described in "#8: Revealing All of PHP's Settings" on page 21). Page through the output, searching for your library. For example, if MySQL is enabled, you'll see a section like this:

```
mysql

MySQL Support => enabled
...
```

If this doesn't work out for you, or you think it's a little slow, there are other things you can try.

An extension adds new functions to PHP—for example, cURL adds functions such as `cURL_init()` and `cURL_setopt()`, Mcrypt adds `mcrypt_encrypt()` and `mcrypt_decrypt()`, and so on. But let's say that Mcrypt *isn't* installed. In that case, PHP doesn't know anything about `mcrypt_decrypt()`—it's just an undefined function.

You can take advantage of this by using the PHP `function_exists()` function. Try this script to detect the MySQL extension:

```php
<?php
if (function_exists(mysql_connect)) {
   print 'MySQL present';
} else {
   print 'MySQL not present';
}
?>
```

Asking Your Hosting Company to Load Extensions

If you're not running your own webserver, as is the case with most people, chances are that you're at the mercy of your web host. Because you don't have root access, you can't install the libraries yourself. In this case, you must request the server administrators to put them in for you. When making your request, be sure that you are very specific; otherwise, you may not get the right version or even the correct extension.

Some companies will do it cheerfully. Others require you to pay a fee to be moved over to a high-powered server with more extensions. And still others will say, "What you have is all we provide. We don't offer custom builds."

If you can't get the extensions you need, you'll either have to live without them or move to another hosting company.

NOTE   *Even if you own the server, it's often easier to ask tech support to install new extensions, if you can get them to do it. That way, should something break during the installation, they'll actually be able to fix it (in theory).*

Installing Extensions with a Web-Based Control Panel

Entire leased servers frequently come with a control panel that allows you to carry out common webmaster tasks via your web browser, such as restarting the Apache service or rebooting the server.

These control panels sometimes allow you to recompile Apache or PHP automatically, using checkboxes or drop-down menus to select the extensions you want to add to PHP. For example, WHM (a common, if slightly troublesome control panel) has the option to "Update Apache," which allows you to reinstall Apache and PHP along with whatever extensions you require.

NOTE   *If your server doesn't come preinstalled with a control panel, you can usually pay a small fee to have one installed.*

Installing an Extension Manually

Recompiling PHP is the Unix way of saying that you're reinstalling PHP and adding the extensions you need at the same time. To those unfamiliar with Unix administration, recompiling PHP can be somewhat challenging.

It's best to start out experimenting with a local Apache server away from a production environment. You can really mess up a live server, so not only do you want to make sure you have some tech support handy in case something goes wrong, you also want to make sure that you've seen some of the things that can go wrong. If you feel completely unprepared for the task, you should get someone to help you.

Getting a library to work with PHP is a two-step process: First, you have to install the libraries for the extensions, and then you must make PHP recognize those extensions.

Installing Libraries

The actual steps involved in installing an extension vary depending on what library you want to use. I can give you a rough overview as to how to do it, but make sure to look for any tutorials on the library's download page and read all the README files before you do anything. If you want a detailed explanation of how it all fits together, you may want to look at the explanation of compiling software in *How Linux Works* by Brian Ward (No Starch Press, 2004).

The general steps are as follows:

1. **Log in to your server as root or as a user with the rights to install new programs.**

2. **Download the library archive to the root directory of your server.** A quick Google search for the library's name and PHP (such as *mcrypt php*) will usually bring you to the library's home page, where you'll find the source files. They'll usually be gzipped and tarred to save on storage space and will look something like *libraryfilename.tar.gz.*

3. **Extract the contents of the archive.** A *tar archive* is a bundle of files and directories. On top of this, the entire archive is compressed with the Gzip package, hence the .gz extension at the very end. Therefore, you can think of a .tar.gz file in the same way as a .zip file, except that .tar.gz is done in two separate stages, with two different programs.

   However, you don't actually have to explicitly run both, because GNU tar knows how to run the decompresser. To extract the contents of your tar file, type `tar zxvf libraryfilename.tar.gz` at the command prompt. You'll get a list of all the files and directories being extracted. Most archives create a tree under one top-level directory, so look for that.

4. **Change to the library's installed directory by typing `cd directoryname`.** If you don't remember or didn't catch the name from the previous step, it's usually the name of the library—`cd cURL`, for example. (The directory name is case-specific, by the way, so *cURL* is different from *CURL*.)

5. **Run the `configure` command to see if all the ingredients are present to complete the install on this machine.** Because of the many different types of Unix, installing a package on it takes some serious know-how. Fortunately, the `configure` command can do most of the dirty work for

you, looking through your server's settings and guessing at the correct values needed to install this program. Type `./configure` at the prompt.

Some extensions require you to put additional flags after the `configure` command in order to get it to work properly. For example, the Mcrypt extension requires you to type `./configure --disable-nls --disable-posix-threads` in order to guarantee compatibility with Apache. Since this is library-specific, look through the tutorials and README files to see if there are any specific configure flags you need to set for your package.

6. **Build and install the package.** In Unix, `make` is a standard utility for compiling and installing a package. First, type `make` to compile the package. You'll see the commands that build the package as they are run. Then, type `make check` to run any self-tests that come with the package (sometimes there are no tests, so don't worry about those cases). Finally, type `make install` to install the extension. The install process appears onscreen. When it's done, your extension will be installed.

7. **Create a `phpinfo()` script.** Oh, you thought you were finished? Sorry, chief, but all you've done is to install the extension on your server. Now you have to actually reinstall PHP and tell it where the extension is and how to use it.

`phpinfo()` (see "#8: Revealing All of PHP's Settings" on page 21) gives you the full settings of your server. About a third of the way down on the first page of your `phpinfo()` script, you will find a section that says *Configure Command*. In it, there will be a cryptic list of things that looks something like this:

```
'./configure' '--with-apxs=/usr/local/apache/bin/apxs' '--with-xml' '--
enable-bcmath' '--enable-calendar' '--enable-ftp' '--enable-magic-quotes'
'--with-mysql' '--enable-discard-path' '--with-pear' '--enable-sockets' '-
-enable-track-vars' '--enable-versioning' '--with-zlib'
```

If you want to reinstall PHP as you currently have it, this would be the command you'd use—almost. First, remove the single quotes around the `configure` command to give you something like this:

```
./configure '--with-apxs=/usr/local/apache/bin/apxs' '--with-xml' '--
enable-bcmath' '--enable-calendar' '--enable-ftp' '--enable-magic-quotes'
'--with-mysql' '--enable-discard-path' '--with-pear' '--enable-sockets' '-
-enable-track-vars' '--enable-versioning' '--with-zlib'
```

The purpose of this step is that when you add an extension such as GD, you don't want to lose the existing extensions you already have installed. Copy this configure information into a text file, and then add appropriate `--with` statements to the end of it. For example, if you were adding Mcrypt to this server, you'd add `--with-mcrypt` to the end of it. Check the extension documentation to find the right `--with` parameter.

If you've overridden the tar directory structure and placed your library into a folder that's not the default, you'll need to add the path to the `--with` *flag so that PHP can find it. This has happened in the apxs (Apache Extension Tool Synopsis) library in our example above, and the* `--with-apxs=/usr/local/apache/bin/apxs` *flag tells PHP that apxs is stored in the /usr/local/apache/bin/apxs directory.*

8. **Fetch and unpack a new PHP source distribution; then change to that directory.** You can unpack the PHP source code just as you did for the library source code previously. If you already have a previous source code tree of PHP, you can use that, but run `make clean` there beforehand.

9. **Copy the** `configure` **command you created earlier from your text file, paste it onto the command prompt, and press ENTER to run it.** This reconfigures PHP with the new library, preserving any old libraries.

10. **Make PHP.** Run `make`, and then run `make install`. There will be a long wait as each command builds and installs all of PHP's components.

If you have made any changes to your .ini files, as shown earlier in this chapter, they may be overwritten with the defaults when PHP is recompiled. Take a look afterward to verify that your settings have been preserved.

11. **Restart Apache.** Run the `apachectl graceful` command.

12. **Test PHP.** First, try running a generic "Hello, world!" script to ensure that PHP is up and running without error, and then try running a couple of library-specific functions to see whether the new library works properly.

What Can Go Wrong?

There are so many things that can go wrong during the build process that it's almost impossible to list them all. Although many errors are complicated, and many of them are library specific so that you will need to seek specific advice, three common problems pop up all the time.

The first major problem that could happen is that your distribution or release may not have the software development packages installed. You need the C compiler and various "development" versions of many other libraries so you can build code against them.

Second, you may need to configure PHP using a `--with` parameter that has an explicit path; for example, `--with-mcrypt=/usr/lib/mcrypt`.

The other common glitch is that you could have configured the extension's library package incorrectly. As mentioned earlier, you should configure Mcrypt with the `--disable-nls --disable-posix-threads` flags; otherwise, you may crash Apache. Other libraries require similar tweaking in order to work smoothly with PHP and Apache. Check the FAQs, man pages, and README files for details.

3

PHP SECURITY

When offering an Internet service, you must always keep security in mind as you develop your code. It may appear that most PHP scripts aren't sensitive to security concerns; this is mainly due to the large number of inexperienced programmers working in the language. However, there is no reason for you to have an inconsistent security policy based on a rough guess at your code's significance. The moment you put anything financially interesting on your server, it becomes likely that someone will try to casually hack it. Create a forum program or any sort of shopping cart, and the probability of attack rises to a dead certainty.

Here are a few general security guidelines.

Don't trust forms.

Hacking forms is trivial. Yes, by using a silly JavaScript trick, you may be able to limit your *form* to allow only the numbers 1 through 5 in a rating field. The moment someone turns JavaScript off in their browser or posts custom form data, your client-side validation flies out the window.

Users interact with your scripts primarily through form parameters, and therefore they're the biggest security risk. What's the lesson? *Always validate the data that gets passed to any PHP script in the PHP script.* "Verification Strategies" on page 46 shows how to validate discrete data. In this chapter, we show you how to analyze and protect against cross-site scripting (XSS) attacks, which can hijack your user's credentials (and worse). You'll also see how to prevent the MySQL injection attacks that can taint or destroy your data.

Don't trust users.

Assume that every piece of data your website gathers is laden with harmful code. Sanitize every piece, even if you're positive that nobody would ever try to attack your site. Paranoia pays off.

Turn off global variables.

The biggest security hole you can have is having the `register_globals` configuration parameter enabled. Mercifully, it's turned off by default in PHP 4.2 and later. Refer to "#14: Turning Off Registered Global Variables" on page 25 to disable this setting.

Novice programmers view registered globals as a convenience, but they don't realize how dangerous this setting is. A server with global variables enabled automatically assigns global variables to any form parameters. For an idea of how this works and why this is dangerous, let's look at an example.

Let's say that you have a script named *process.php* that enters form data into your user database. The original form looked like this:

```
<input name="username" type="text" size="15" maxlength="64">
```

When running process.php, PHP with registered globals enabled places the value of this parameter into the `$username` variable. This saves some typing over accessing them through `$_POST['username']` or `$_GET['username']`. Unfortunately, this also leaves you open to security problems, because PHP sets a variable for *any* value sent to the script via a GET or POST parameter, and that is a big problem if you didn't explicitly initialize the variable and you don't want someone to manipulate it.

Take the script below, for example—if the `$authorized` variable is `true`, it shows confidential data to the user. Under normal circumstances, the `$authorized` variable is set to `true` *only* if the user has been properly authenticated via the hypothetical `authenticated_user()` function. But if you have `register_globals` active, anyone could send a GET parameter such as `authorized=1` to override this:

```php
<?php
// Define $authorized = true only if user is authenticated
if (authenticated_user()) {
    $authorized = true;
}
?>
```

The moral of the story is that you should follow the procedure in "#25: Fetching Form Variables Consistently and Safely" on page 47 to access form data. It doesn't sound like it would happen often, but exploits for `register_globals` are second only to XSS attacks in PHP. Furthermore, global variables can lead to much subtler issues that *will* cause bugs later on in your code.

Recommended Security Configuration Options

There are several PHP configuration settings that affect security features. Here are the ones that I use for production servers (see Chapter 2 for how to set them):

- `register_globals` set to *off*. See the previous discussion.
- `safe_mode` set to *off*. This parameter doesn't really make anything safe.
- `display_errors` set to *off*. This is *visible* error reporting that sends a message to the user's browser if something goes wrong. For production servers, use error logging instead (see "#11: Suppressing All Error Messages" on page 24). Development servers can enable error logging as long as they're behind a firewall.
- Disable these functions: `system()`, `exec()`, `passthru()`, `shell_exec()`, `proc_open()`, and `popen()`. See "#17: Shutting Down Specific Functions" on page 27.
- `open_basedir` set for both the /tmp directory (so that session information can be stored) and the web root so that scripts cannot access files outside a selected area.
- `expose_php` set to *off*. This feature adds a PHP signature that includes the version number to the Apache headers. Why would you want to do that?
- `allow_url_fopen` set to *off*. This isn't strictly necessary if you're careful about how you access files in your code—that is, you validate all input parameters.
- `allow_url_include` set to *off*. There's really no sane reason for anyone to want to access include files via HTTP.

In general, if you find code that wants to use these features, you shouldn't trust it. Be especially careful of anything that wants to use a function such as `system()`—it's almost certainly flawed.

With these settings now behind us, let's look at some specific attacks and the methods that will help you protect your server.

#19: SQL Injection Attacks

Because the queries that PHP passes to MySQL databases are written in the powerful SQL programming language, you run the risk of someone attempting an *SQL injection attack* by using MySQL in web query parameters. By inserting malicious SQL code fragments into form parameters, an attacker attempts to break into (or disable) your server.

Let's say that you have a form parameter that you eventually place into a variable named $product, and you create some SQL like this:

```
$sql = "select * from pinfo where product = '$product'";
```

If that parameter came straight from the form, use database-specific escapes with PHP's native functions, like this:

```
$sql = 'Select * from pinfo where product = '"' .
    mysql_real_escape_string($product) . '"';
```

If you don't, someone might just decide to throw this fragment into the form parameter:

```
39'; DROP pinfo; SELECT 'FOO
```

Then the result of $sql is:

```
select product from pinfo where product = '39'; DROP pinfo; SELECT 'FOO'
```

Because the semicolon is MySQL's statement delimiter, the database processes these three statements:

```
select * from pinfo where product = '39'
DROP pinfo
SELECT 'FOO'
```

Well, there goes your table.

Note that this particular syntax won't actually work with PHP and MySQL, because the mysql_query() function allows just one statement to be processed per request. However, a subquery will still work.

To prevent SQL injection attacks, do two things:

- Always validate all parameters. For example, if something needs to be a number, make sure that it's a number.

- Always use the mysql_real_escape_string() function on data to escape any quotes or double quotes in your data.

NOTE   *To automatically escape any form data, you can turn on Magic Quotes. See "#15: Enabling Magic Quotes" on page 26.*

Some MySQL damage can be avoided by restricting your MySQL user privileges. Any MySQL account can be restricted to only do certain kinds of queries on selected tables. For example, you could create a MySQL user who can select rows but nothing else. However, this is not terribly useful for dynamic data, and, furthermore, if you have sensitive customer information, it might be possible for someone to have access to some data that you didn't intend to make available. For example, a user accessing account data could try to inject some code that accesses another account number instead of the one assigned to the current session.

#20: Preventing Basic XSS Attacks

XSS stands for *cross-site scripting*. Unlike most attacks, this exploit works on the client side. The most basic form of XSS is to put some JavaScript in user-submitted content to steal the data in a user's cookie. Since most sites use cookies and sessions to identify visitors, the stolen data can then be used to impersonate that user—which is deeply troublesome when it's a typical user account, and downright disastrous if it's the administrative account. If you don't use cookies or session IDs on your site, your users aren't vulnerable, but you should still be aware of how this attack works.

Unlike MySQL injection attacks, XSS attacks are difficult to prevent. Yahoo!, eBay, Apple, and Microsoft have all been affected by XSS. Although the attack doesn't involve PHP, you *can* use PHP to strip user data in order to prevent attacks. To stop an XSS attack, you have to restrict and filter the data a user submits to your site. It is for this precise reason that most online bulletin boards don't allow the use of HTML tags in posts and instead replace them with custom tag formats such as [b] and [linkto].

Let's look at a simple script that illustrates how to prevent some of these attacks. For a more complete solution, use SafeHTML, discussed later in this chapter.

```
function transform_HTML($string, $length = null) {
// Helps prevent XSS attacks

    // Remove dead space.
    $string = trim($string);

    // Prevent potential Unicode codec problems.
    $string = utf8_decode($string);

    // HTMLize HTML-specific characters.
    $string = htmlentities($string, ENT_NOQUOTES);
    $string = str_replace("#", "&#35;", $string);
    $string = str_replace("%", "&#37;", $string);

    $length = intval($length);
    if ($length > 0) {
        $string = substr($string, 0, $length);
    }
    return $string;
}
```

This function transforms HTML-specific characters into HTML literals. A browser renders any HTML run through this script as text with no markup. For example, consider this HTML string:

```
<STRONG>Bold Text</STRONG>
```

Normally, this HTML would render as follows:

```
Bold Text
```

However, when run through `transform_HTML()`, it renders as the original input. The reason is that the tag characters are HTML entities in the processed string. The resulting string from `HTML()` in plaintext looks like this:

```
&lt;STRONG&gt;Bold Text&lt;/STRONG&gt;
```

The essential piece of this function is the `htmlentities()` function call that transforms <, >, and & into their entity equivalents of <, >, and &. Although this takes care of the most common attacks, experienced XSS hackers have another sneaky trick up their sleeve: Encoding their malicious scripts in hexadecimal or UTF-8 instead of normal ASCII text, hoping to circumvent your filters. They can send the code along as a GET variable in the URL, saying, "Hey, this is hexadecimal code, but could you run it for me anyway?" A hexadecimal example looks something like this:

```
<a href="http://host/a.php?variable=%22%3e %3c%53%43%52%49%50%54%3e%44
%6f%73%6f%6d%65%74%68%69%6e%67%6d%61%6c%69%63%69%6f%75%73%3c%2f%53%43%52
%49%50%54%3e">
```

But when the browser renders that information, it turns out to be:

```
<a href="http://host/a.php?variable="> <SCRIPT>Dosomethingmalicious</SCRIPT>
```

To prevent this, `transform_HTML()` takes the additional steps of converting # and % signs into their entity, shutting down hex attacks, and converting UTF-8–encoded data.

Finally, just in case someone tries to overload a string with a very long input, hoping to crash something, you can add an optional `$length` parameter to trim the string to the maximum length you specify.

#21: Using SafeHTML

The problem with the previous script is that it *is* simple, and it does not allow for any kind of user markup. Unfortunately, there are hundreds of ways to try to sneak JavaScript past someone's filters, and short of stripping all HTML from someone's input, there's no way of stopping it.

Currently, there's no single script that's guaranteed to be unbreakable, though there are some that are better than most. As you'll learn in more detail in "Verification Strategies" on page 46, there are two approaches to security, whitelisting and blacklisting, and whitelisting tends to be less complicated and more effective.

One whitelisting solution is the SafeHTML anti-XSS parser from PixelApes.

SafeHTML is smart enough to recognize valid HTML, so it can hunt and strip any dangerous tags. It does its parsing with another package called HTMLSax.

To install and use SafeHTML, do the following:

1. Go to http://pixel-apes.com/safehtml/?page=safehtml and download the latest version of SafeHTML.

2. Put the files in the classes directory on your server. This directory contains everything that SafeHTML and HTMLSax need to function.

3. Include the SafeHTML class file (safehtml.php) in your script.

4. Create a new SafeHTML object called $safehtml.

5. Sanitize your data with the $safehtml->parse() method.

Here's a complete example:

```php
<?php
/* If you're storing the HTMLSax3.php in the /classes directory, along
   with the safehtml.php script, define XML_HTMLSAX3 as a null string. */
define(XML_HTMLSAX3, '');
// Include the class file.
require_once('classes/safehtml.php');
// Define some sample bad code.
$data = "This data would raise an alert <script>alert('XSS Attack')</script>";
// Create a safehtml object.
$safehtml = new safehtml();
// Parse and sanitize the data.
$safe_data = $safehtml->parse($data);
// Display result.
echo 'The sanitized data is <br />' . $safe_data;
?>
```

If you want to sanitize any other data in your script, you don't have to create a new object; just use the $safehtml->parse() method throughout your script.

What Can Go Wrong?

The biggest mistake you can make is assuming that this class completely shuts down XSS attacks. SafeHTML is a fairly complex script that checks for almost everything, but nothing is guaranteed. You still want to do the parameter validation that applies to your site. For example, this class doesn't check the length of a given variable to ensure that it fits into a database field. It doesn't check for buffer overflow problems.

XSS hackers are creative and use a variety of approaches to try to accomplish their objectives. Just look at RSnake's XSS tutorial at http://ha.ckers .org/xss.html to see how many ways there are to try to sneak code past someone's filters. The SafeHTML project has good programmers working overtime to try to stop XSS attacks, and it has a solid approach, but there's no guarantee that someone won't come up with some weird and fresh approach that could short-circuit its filters.

NOTE *For an example of the powerful effects of XSS attacks, check out http://namb.la/popular/ tech.html, which shows a step-by-step approach to creating the JavaScript XSS worm that overloaded the MySpace servers.*

#22: Protecting Data with a One-Way Hash

This script performs a one-way transformation on data—in other words, it can make a hash signature of someone's password, but you can't ever decrypt it and go back to the original password. Why would you want to do that? The application is in storing passwords. An administrator doesn't need to know users' passwords—in fact, it's a good idea that only the user knows his or her password. The system (and the system alone) should be able to identify a correct password; this has been the Unix password security model for years. One-way password security works as follows:

1. When a user or administrator creates or changes an account password, the system hashes the password and stores the result. The host system discards the plaintext password.
2. When the user logs in to a system via any means, the entered password is again hashed.
3. The host system throws away the plaintext password entered.
4. This newly hashed password is compared against the stored hash.
5. If the hashed passwords match, then the system grants access.

The host system does this without ever knowing the original password; in fact, the original value is completely irrelevant. As a side effect, should someone break into your system and steal your password database, the intruder will have a bunch of hashed passwords without any way of reversing them to find the originals. Of course, given enough time, computer power, and poorly chosen user passwords, an attacker could probably use a dictionary attack to figure out the passwords. Therefore, don't make it easy for people to get their hands on your password database, and if someone does, have everyone change their passwords.

ENCRYPTION VS. HASHING

Technically speaking, this process is not encryption. It is a hash, which is different from encryption for two reasons:

- Unlike in encryption, data cannot be *decrypted*.
- It's possible (but extremely unlikely) that two different strings will produce the same hash. There's no guarantee that a hash is unique, so don't try to use a hash as something like a unique key in a database.

```
function hash_ish($string) {
    return md5($string);
}
```

The md5() function returns a 32-character hexadecimal string, based on the RSA Data Security Inc. Message-Digest Algorithm (also known, conveniently enough, as MD5). You can then insert that 32-character string into your database, compare it against other md5'd strings, or just adore its 32-character perfection.

Hacking the Script

It is virtually impossible to decrypt MD5 data. That is, it's *very* hard. However, you still need good passwords, because it's still easy to make a database of hashes for the entire dictionary. There are online MD5 dictionaries where you can enter **06d80eb0c50b49a509b49f2424e8c805** and get a result of "dog." Thus, even though MD5s can't *technically* be decrypted, they're still vulnerable—and if someone gets your password database, you can be sure that they'll be consulting an MD5 dictionary. Thus, it's in your best interests when creating password-based systems that the passwords are long (a minimum of six characters and preferably eight) and contain both letters and numbers. And make sure that the password isn't in the dictionary.

#23: Encrypting Data with Mcrypt

MD5 hashes work just fine if you never need to see your data in readable form. Unfortunately, that's not always an option—if you offer to store someone's credit card information in encrypted format, you need to decrypt it at some later point.

One of the easiest solutions is the Mcrypt module, an add-in for PHP that allows high-grade encryption. The Mcrypt library offers more than 30 ciphers to use in encryption and the possibility of a passphrase that ensures that *only* you (or, optionally, your users) can decrypt data. To use Mcrypt, recompile PHP data with Mcrypt support, as explained in "#18: Adding Extensions to PHP" on page 27.

Let's see some hands-on use. The following script contains functions that use Mcrypt to encrypt and decrypt data:

```php
<?php

$data = "Stuff you want encrypted";
$key = "Secret passphrase used to encrypt your data";
$cipher = MCRYPT_SERPENT;
$mode = MCRYPT_MODE_CBC;

function encrypt($data, $key, $cipher, $mode) {
// Encrypt data

return (string)
        base64_encode
            (
            mcrypt_encrypt
                (
                $cipher,
                substr(md5($key),0,mcrypt_get_key_size($cipher, $mode)),
                $data,
                $mode,
                substr(md5($key),0,mcrypt_get_block_size($cipher, $mode))
                )
            );
```

```
}

function decrypt($data, $key, $cipher, $mode) {
// Decrypt data
    return (string)
            mcrypt_decrypt
                (
                $cipher,
                substr(md5($key),0,mcrypt_get_key_size($cipher, $mode)),
                base64_decode($data),
                $mode,
                substr(md5($key),0,mcrypt_get_block_size($cipher, $mode))
                );
}

?>
```

The mcrypt() function requires several pieces of information:

- The data to be encrypted.

- The passphrase used to encrypt and unlock your data, also known as the *key*.

- The *cipher* used to encrypt the data, which is the specific algorithm used to encrypt the data. This script uses MCRYPT_SERPENT, but you can choose from an array of fancy-sounding ciphers, including MCRYPT_TWOFISH192, MCRYPT_RC2, MCRYPT_DES, and MCRYPT_LOKI97.

NOTE *To find out which ciphers are available on your server, check out "#8: Revealing All of PHP's Settings" on page 21, and then head to the "Mcrypt" section on the phpinfo() page. If Mcrypt is available, you will see two sections: "Supported Cipher" and "Supported Modes." Use them, exactly as written, to encrypt your data.*

- The *mode* used to encrypt the data. There are several modes you can use, including Electronic Codebook and Cipher Feedback. This script uses MCRYPT_MODE_CBC, Cipher Block Chaining.

- An *initialization vector*—also known as an *IV*, or a *seed*—an additional bit of binary data used to seed the encryption algorithm. That is, it's something extra thrown in to make the algorithm harder to crack.

- The length of the string needed for the key and IV, which vary by cipher and block. Use the mcrypt_get_key_size() and mcrypt_get_block_size() functions to find the appropriate length; then trim the key value to the appropriate length with a handy substr() function. (If the key is shorter than the required value, don't worry—Mcrypt pads it with zeros.)

If someone steals both your data and your passphrase, they can just cycle through the ciphers until finding the one that works. Thus, we apply the additional security of using the md5() function on the key before we use it, so even having both data and passphrase won't get the intruder what she wants.

An intruder would need the function, the data, and the passphrase all at once—and if *that* is the case, they probably have complete access to your server, and you're hosed anyway.

There's a small data storage format problem here. Mcrypt returns its encrypted data in an ugly binary format that causes horrific errors when you try to store it in certain MySQL fields. Therefore, we use the base64encode() and base64decode() functions to transform the data into a SQL-compatible alphabetical format and retrieve rows.

Hacking the Script

In addition to experimenting with various encryption methods, you can add some convenience to this script. For example, rather than providing the key and mode every time, you could declare them as global constants in an included file (see "#1: Including Another File as a Part of Your Script" on page 2).

#24: Generating Random Passwords

Random (but difficult-to-guess) strings are important in user security. For example, if someone loses a password and you're using MD5 hashes, you won't be able to, nor should you want to, look it up. Instead, you should generate a secure random password and send that to the user. Another application for random number generation is creating activation links in order to access your site's services. Here is a function that creates a password:

```php
<?php
 function make_password($num_chars) {
    if ((is_numeric($num_chars)) &&
        ($num_chars > 0) &&
        (! is_null($num_chars))) {

        $password = '';
        $accepted_chars = 'abcdefghijklmnopqrstuvwxyz1234567890';

        // Seed the generator if necessary.
        srand(((int)((double)microtime()*1000003)) );

        for ($i=0; $i<=$num_chars; $i++) {
            $random_number = rand(0, (strlen($accepted_chars) -1));
            $password .= $accepted_chars[$random_number] ;
        }

        return $password;
    }
}
?>
```

Using the Script

The make_password() function returns a string, so all you need to do is supply the length of the string as an argument:

```php
<?php
$fifteen_character_password = make_password(15);
?>
```

The function works as follows:

1. The function makes sure that $num_chars is a positive nonzero integer.
2. The function initializes the $password variable to an empty string.
3. The function initializes the $accepted_chars variable to the list of characters the password may contain. This script uses all lowercase letters and the numbers 0 through 9, but you can choose any set of characters you like.
4. The random number generator needs a seed, so it gets a bunch of random-like values. (This isn't strictly necessary on PHP 4.2 and later.)
5. The function loops $num_chars times, one iteration for each character in the password to generate.
6. For each new character, the script looks at the length of $accepted_chars, chooses a number between 0 and the length, and adds the character at that index in $accepted_chars to $password.
7. After the loop completes, the function returns $password.

4

WORKING WITH FORMS

Forms are how your users talk to your scripts. To get the most out of PHP, you must master forms. The first thing you need to understand is that although PHP makes it easy to access form data, you must be careful of how you work with the data.

Security Measures: Forms Are Not Trustworthy

A common mistake that novices make is to trust the data provided by an HTML form. If you have a drop-down menu that only allows the user to enter one of three values, you must still check those values. As mentioned in Chapter 3, you also cannot rely on JavaScript to stop people from sending whatever they like to your server.

Your site's users can write their own form in HTML to use against your server; users can also bypass the browser entirely and use automatic tools to interact with web scripts. You should assume that people will mess around with parameters when you put a script on the Web, because they might be trying to discover an easier way to use your site (though they could be attempting something altogether less beneficial).

To ensure that your server is safe, you must verify all data that your scripts receive.

Verification Strategies

There are two approaches to checking form data: blacklisting and whitelisting.

Blacklisting is the process of trying to filter out all bad data by assuming that form submissions are valid and then explicitly seeking out bad data. In general, this technique is ineffective and inefficient. For example, let's say that you're trying to eliminate all "bad" characters from a string, such as quotes. You might search for and replace quotation marks, but the problem is that there will *always* be bad characters you didn't think of. In general, blacklisting assumes that most of the data you receive is friendly.

A better assumption to make about form data you're receiving is that it's inherently malicious; thus, you should filter your data in order to *accept* only valid data submissions. This technique is called *whitelisting*. For example, if a string should consist of only alphanumeric characters, then you can check it against a regular expression that matches only an entire string of A-Za-z0-9. Whitelisting may also include forcing data to a known range of values or changing the type of a value. Here is an overview of a few specific tactics:

- If the value should be a number, use the is_numeric() function to verify the value. You can force a value to an integer using the intval() function. If the value should be an array, use is_array().

- If the value should be a string, use is_string(). To force it, use strval().

- If the value should be null, use is_null().

- If the value should be defined, use isset().

WHITELISTING INTEGERS

Here's a typical example of how you might whitelist for a numeric value. If the data is not numeric, then you use a default value of zero (of course, this assumes that zero is an acceptable value):

```
if (! is_numeric($data)) {
    // Use a default of 0.
    $data = 0;
}
```

In the case of integers, there is an alternative if you know that all integer values are safe. Using $data = intval($data); forces $data to its integral value. This technique is called *typecasting*.

Using $_POST, $_GET, $_REQUEST, and $_FILES to Access Form Data

In Chapter 2, we showed you how to turn off the register_globals setting that automatically sets global variables based on form data.

To shut down this dangerous setting, refer to "#14: Turning Off Registered Global Variables" on page 25. How do you use $_POST, $_FILES, and $_GET to retrieve form data? Read on.

#25: Fetching Form Variables Consistently and Safely

You should pull form data from *predefined server variables*. All data passed on to your web page via a posted form is automatically stored in a large array called $_POST, and all GET data is stored in a large array called $_GET. File upload information is stored in a special array called $_FILES (see "#54: Uploading Images to a Directory" on page 97 for more information on files). In addition, there is a combined variable called $_REQUEST.

To access the username field from a POST method form, use $_POST['username']. Use $_GET['username'] if the username is in the URL. If you don't care where the value came from, use $_REQUEST['username'].

```php
<?php

$post_value = $_POST['post_value'];
$get_value = $_GET['get_value'];
$some_variable = $_REQUEST['some_value'];

?>
```

$_REQUEST is a union of the $_GET, $_POST, and $_COOKIE arrays. If you have two or more values of the same parameter name, be careful of which one PHP uses. The default order is cookie, POST, then GET.

There has been some debate on how safe $_REQUEST is, but there shouldn't be. Because all of its sources come from the outside world (the user's browser), you need to verify everything in this array that you plan to use, just as you would with the other predefined arrays. The only problems you might have are confusing bugs that might pop up as a result of cookies being included.

#26: Trimming Excess Whitespace

Excess whitespace is a constant problem when working with form data. The trim() function is usually the first tool a programmer turns to, because it removes any excess spaces from the beginning or end of a string. For example, " Wicked Cool PHP   " becomes "Wicked Cool PHP." In fact, it's so handy that you may find yourself using it on almost every available piece of user-inputted, non-array data:

```
$user_input = trim($user_input);
```

But sometimes you have excessive whitespace *inside* a string—when someone may be cutting and copying information from an email, for instance. In that case, you can replace multiple spaces and other whitespace with a single space by using the preg_replace() function. The *reg* stands for *regular expression*, a powerful form of pattern matching that you will see several times in this chapter.

```php
<?php
function remove_whitespace($string) {
    $string = preg_replace('/\s+/', ' ', $string);
    $string = trim($string);
    return $string;
}
?>
```

You'll find many uses for this script outside of form verification. It's great for cleaning up data that comes from other external sources.

#27: Importing Form Variables into an Array

One of the handiest tricks you can use in PHP is not actually a PHP trick but an HTML trick. When a user fills out a form, you'll frequently check the values of several checkboxes. For example, let's say you're taking a survey to see what sorts of movies your site's visitors like, and you'd like to automatically insert those values into a database called customer_preferences. The hard way to do that is to give each checkbox a separate name on the HTML form, as shown here:

```html
<p>What movies do you like?</p>
<input type="checkbox" name="action" value="yes"> Action
<input type="checkbox" name="drama" value="yes"> Drama
<input type="checkbox" name="comedy" value="yes"> Comedy
<input type="checkbox" name="romance" value="yes"> Romance
```

Unfortunately, when you process the form on the next page, you'll need a series of if/then loops to check the data—one loop to check the value of $action, one to check the value of $drama, and so forth. Adding a new checkbox to the HTML form results in yet another if/then loop to the processing page.

A great way to simplify this procedure is to store all of the checkbox values in a single array by adding [] after the name, like this (see Figure 4-1):

```html
<form action="process.php" method="post">
<p>What is your name?</p>
<p><input type="text" name="customer_name"></p>

<p>What movies do you like?</p>
<p><input type="checkbox" name="movie_type[]" value="action"> Action
<input type="checkbox" name="movie_type[]" value="drama"> Drama
```

```
<input type="checkbox" name="movie_type[]" value="comedy"> Comedy
<input type="checkbox" name="movie_type[]" value="romance"> Romance</p>
<input type="submit">
</form>
```

What is your name?

What movies do you like?

☐ Action ☐ Drama ☐ Comedy ☐ Romance

Submit Query

Figure 4-1: A form with an array of checkboxes

When PHP gets the data from a form like this, it stores the checked values in a single array. You can loop through the array this way:

```
<?php
$movie_type = $_POST["movie_type"];
$customer_name = strval($_POST["customer_name"]);

if (is_array($movie_type)) {
    foreach ($movie_type as $key => $value) {
        print "$customer_name likes $value movies.<br>";
    }
}

?>
```

Not only does this technique work for checkboxes, but it's extremely handy for processing arbitrary numbers of rows. For example, let's say we have a shopping menu where we want to show all the items in a given category. Although we may not know how many items will be in a category, the customer should be able to enter a quantity into a text box for all items he wants to buy and add all of the items with a single click.

Let's access product name and ID data in the product_info MySQL table described in the appendix to build the form as follows:

```
<?php
/* Insert code for connecting to $db here. */

$category = "shoes";
/* Retrieve products from the database. */
$sql = "SELECT product_name, product_id
        FROM product_info
        WHERE category = '$category'";

$result = @mysql_query($sql, $db) or die;
```

```
/* Initialize variables. */
$order_form = ""; /* Will contain product form data */
$i = 1;

print '<form action="addtocart.php" method="post">';

while($row = mysql_fetch_array($result)) {
    // Loop through the results from the MySQL query.
    $product_name = stripslashes($row['product_name']);
    $product_id = $row['product_id'];

    // Add the row to the order form.
    print "<input type=\"hidden\" name=\"product_id[$i]\" value=\"$product_id\
">";
    print "<input type=\"text\" name=\"quantity[$i]\"
    size=\"2\" value=\"0\"> $product_name<br />";

    $i++;
}

print '<input type="submit" name="add" value="Add to Cart"></form>';


?>
```

To process the form, you need to examine the two arrays passed to the processing script—one array containing all of the product IDs ($product_id) and another containing the corresponding values from the quantity text boxes ($quantity). It doesn't matter how many items are displayed on the page; $product_id[123] contains the product ID for the 123rd item displayed and $quantity[123] holds the number the customer entered into the corresponding text box.

The processing script addtocart.php is as follows:

```
<?php

$product_id = $_POST["product_id"];
$quantity = $_POST["quantity"];

if (is_array($quantity)) {
    foreach ($quantity as $key => $item_qty) {
        $item_qty = intval($item_qty);
        if ($item_qty > 0) {
            $id = $product_id[$key];
            print "You added $item_qty of Product ID $id.<br>";
        }
    }
}

?>
```

As you can see, this script depends wholly on using the index from the $quantity array ($key) for the $product_id array.

#28: Making Sure a Response Is One of a Set of Given Values

As I told you earlier, you can *never* assume that the data passed on by a form is safe. Let's look at this simple form item:

```
<SELECT NAME="card_type">
<OPTION value="visa">Visa</OPTION>
<OPTION value="amex">American Express</OPTION>
<OPTION value="mastercard">MasterCard</OPTION>
</SELECT>
```

How do you ensure that the data you're looking at is really Visa, American Express, or MasterCard? Simple: You store the data in array keys and then look at the array to make sure that there's an exact match. Here's an example:

```php
<?php

$credit_cards = array(
    "amex"          => true,
    "visa"          => true,
    "mastercard"    => true,
);
$card_type = $_POST["card_type"];
if ($credit_cards[$card_type]) {
    print "$card_type is a valid credit card.";
} else {
    print "$card_type is not a valid credit card.";
}
```

Hacking the Script

One advantage of this method of data storage is that you can temporarily disable an item by changing its value to false. You can also alter the script slightly to provide both verbose values and data values. For example, you may store American Express cards in your database as *amex*, but when the name of the card is displayed on the screen you want it to show up as *American Express*.

In that case, you can use a map to remember what's what by storing the database value as the key in the array and the display name as the value. The following example demonstrates that technique.

```php
<?php
$credit_cards = array(
    "amex"          => "American Express",
    "visa"          => "Visa",
    "mastercard"    => "MasterCard",
);
$card_type = $_POST["card_type"];
if (count($credit_cards[$credit_card_type]) > 0) {
    print "Your payment type: $credit_cards[$card_type].";
} else {
    print "Invalid card type.";
}
```

NOTE *The previous example is extremely useful information to store in a central configuration file.*

#29: Using Multiple Submit Buttons

Occasionally you want a form that does two separate things depending on which button a user clicks—one button updates a post while the other button deletes it. You can put two forms on one page that will send the user to two separate pages, but then you have to worry about inserting redundant information into both forms, not to mention that this would be unbearable to the user.

In HTML, buttons also have values, and you can read those values. Construct your form as follows:

```
<form action="process.php" method="post">
<input name="postid" type="hidden" value="1234">
<input name="action" type="submit" value="Update">
<input name="action" type="submit" value="Delete">
</form>
```

Now, in process.php, access `$_POST['action']` to get the button the user clicked.

#30: Validating a Credit Card

Here's a brief overview of how online credit card transactions work. First, you need to find a *merchant solution* (an online provider, such as Authorize.net or Secpay.com) that provides you with a *merchant account.* This account is like a bank account, except that it allows you to process charges for credit card transactions. The merchant provider typically charges a per-transaction fee for each credit card action.

If you have a physical store that accepts credit cards, you almost certainly have a merchant solution. However, not all merchant solutions offer online transactions. The ones that do offer online transactions give you access to a *payment gateway*, a secure server for processing credit card charges. Usually, the transactions occur via an XML datastream. You can use cURL to exchange XML with the payment gateway (see Chapter 11 for more details).

However, you can do some preliminary form validation work before talking to the payment gateway to save on transactions and transaction fees and possibly speed things for the user if they typed their credit card number incorrectly. It turns out that you can weed out completely incorrect credit card numbers with an easy algorithm. Furthermore, you can even determine a credit card type from a valid number. Keep in mind, though, that passing these tests is no guarantee that a card isn't stolen or canceled or that it belongs to a different person.

```php
<?php
function validate_cc_number($cc_number) {
    /* Validate; return value is card type if valid. */
    $false = false;
    $card_type = "";
    $card_regexes = array(
        "/^4\d{12}(\d\d\d){0,1}$/"    => "visa",
        "/^5[12345]\d{14}$/"          => "mastercard",
        "/^3[47]\d{13}$/"             => "amex",
        "/^6011\d{12}$/"              => "discover",
        "/^30[012345]\d{11}$/"        => "diners",
        "/^3[68]\d{12}$/"             => "diners",
    );

    foreach ($card_regexes as $regex => $type) {
        if (preg_match($regex, $cc_number)) {
            $card_type = $type;
            break;
        }
    }

    if (!$card_type) {
        return $false;
    }

    /* mod 10 checksum algorithm */
    $revcode = strrev($cc_number);
    $checksum = 0;

    for ($i = 0; $i < strlen($revcode); $i++) {
        $current_num = intval($revcode[$i]);
        if ($i & 1) {                /* Odd position */
            $current_num *= 2;
        }
        /* Split digits and add. */
        $checksum += $current_num % 10;
        if ($current_num > 9) {
            $checksum += 1;
        }
    }

    if ($checksum % 10 == 0) {
        return $card_type;
    } else {
        return $false;
    }
}
?>
```

This function has two main stages. The first determines card type, and the second determines whether the card checksum is correct. If the card passes both tests, the return value is the card type as a string. If a card is invalid, you get false (you can change this return value to whatever you like with the $false variable).

The first stage is where the big trick comes in, where we determine the card type and confirm the prefix in one quick step. Credit card numbers follow a certain format. For example, all Visas start with 4 and have 13 or 16 digits, all MasterCards start with 51 through 55 and have 16 digits, and all American Express cards start with 34 or 37 and have 15 digits. These rules are easily expressed in a few regular expressions, and because they are unique rules, we can map the regular expressions to card types in an array called $card_regexes. To check for a valid format, we just cycle through the regular expressions until one matches. When we get a match, we set $card_type and move to the next stage. If no expressions match, we return failure.

The checksum test for the credit card number uses a mod 10 algorithm, a reasonably simple-to-implement check that does the following:

- It starts with a checksum value of 0.
- It runs through the credit card number digit-by-digit from right to left.
- If the current digit has an odd index (that is, every other digit, starting at index 0), the digit is doubled. If the value of the doubled digit is over 9, the two numbers are added together and added to the checksum (so an 8 becomes 16, which becomes 1 + 6, which becomes 7). Otherwise the current (doubled if on an odd index) digit is added to the checksum.
- After running through all the digits, the final checksum must be divisible by 10. If not, the number fails the test.

There are several ways to code this algorithm; the implementation here is on the compact side, but easy enough to follow.

Using the Script

Just feed a string with a number to validate_cc_number() and check the return value. The only thing you should be careful about is nondigits in the string; you should take care of this with preg_replace() before running the function. Here is a snippet that runs the function on several test numbers:

```
$nums = array(
    "3721 0000 0000 000",
    "340000000000009",
    "5500 0000 0000 0004",
    "4111 1111 1111 1111",
    "4222 2222 22222",
    "4007000000027",
    "30000000000004",
    "6011000000000004",
);
```

```
foreach ($nums as $num) {
    /* Remove all non-digits in card number. */
    $num = ereg_replace("[^0-9]", "", $num);

    $t = validate_cc_number($num);
    if ($t) {
        print "$num valid (type: $t).\n";
    } else {
        print "$num invalid.\n";
    }
}
```

Hacking the Script

You can add other major credit cards if you know their format. An excellent resource for other cards is http://www.sitepoint.com/print/card-validation-class-php.

#31: Double-Checking a Credit Card's Expiration Date

When you accept a credit card, you'll need to know whether it has expired. In your HTML, it's best to create a drop-down menu that allows customers to choose their card's expiration date in order to avoid ambiguity in date formats:

```
<select name="cc_month">
<option value="01" >01 : January</option>
        <option value="02" >02 : February</option>
        <option value="03" >03 : March</option>
        <option value="04" >04 : April</option>
        <option value="05" >05 : May</option>
        <option value="06" >06 : June</option>
        <option value="07" >07 : July</option>
        <option value="08" >08 : August</option>
        <option value="09" >09 : September</option>
        <option value="10" >10 : October</option>
        <option value="11" >11 : November</option>
        <option value="12" >12 : December</option>
    </select>
<select name="cc_year">
<?php
    /* Create options for all years up to ten years from now. */
    $y = intval(date("Y"));
    for ($i = $y; $i <= $y + 10; $i++) {
        print "<option value=\"$i\">$i</option>\n";
    }
?>

</select>
```

Now that you have a form for entering an expiration date, you need to validate the data sent by it.

```php
<?php
function check_exp_date($month, $year) {
    /* Get timestamp of midnight on day after expiration month. */
    $exp_ts = mktime(0, 0, 0, $month + 1, 1, $year);

    $cur_ts = time();
    /* Don't validate for dates more than 10 years in future. */
    $max_ts = $cur_ts + (10 * 365 * 24 * 60 * 60);

    if ($exp_ts > $cur_ts && $exp_ts < $max_ts) {
        return true;
    } else {
        return false;
    }
}
?>
```

To check a credit card expiration date, all you have to do is make sure that the date falls between the current date and some date in the future (this function uses 10 years). The best tools for that task are described in Chapter 6, so consider this a sneak preview.

The only trick here is that a credit card becomes invalid after the last day of the month in its expiration date. That is, if a card's expiration date was 06/2005, it actually stopped working on July 1, 2005. Thus, we have to add a month to the given date. This can be a pain because it can also set the actual target date ahead a year, but as you will learn in Chapter 6, the `mktime()` function that we're using here to compute the expiration timestamp automatically compensates for month numbers that are out of range. After computing the expiration timestamp, all you need are the current and maximum timestamps, and validating the expiration time boils down to a pair of simple comparisons.

Using the Script

```php
if (check_exp_date($cc_month, $cc_year)) {
    // Approve the card.
} else {
    // The card has expired.
}
```

#32: Checking Valid Email Addresses

Customers enter all sorts of weird data into email form fields. The script in this section verifies that an email address mostly follows the rules outlined in RFC 2822. This won't prevent someone from entering a false (but RFC-compliant) email address such as leavemealone@nonexistentdomain.com, but it will catch some typos.

NOTE   *If having a valid email address is critical, you need to require user accounts that are activated by links sent only via email. You'll see how to do this in "#65: Using Email to Verify User Accounts" on page 124. This is a fairly extreme measure; if you want more people to share their addresses with you, simply tell users that you won't spam them (and make good on that promise).*

```php
<?php

function is_email($email) {
// Checks for proper email format

    if (! preg_match( '/^[A-Za-z0-9!#$%&\'*+-/=?^_`{|}~]+@[A-Za-z0-9-]+(\.[A-
Za-z0-9-]+)+[A-Za-z]$/', $email)) {
            return false;
    } else {
        return true;
    }
}
?>
```

This script utilizes a regular expression to check whether the given email uses proper email characters (alphabetical, dots, dashes, slashes, and so on), an @ sign in the middle, and at least one dot-something on the end. You can read more on regular expressions in "#39: Regular Expressions" on page 69.

#33: Checking American Phone Numbers

As with email addresses, there's no way to make sure a telephone number is valid outside of making a real telephone call. However, you can validate the number of digits and put it into standard format. The following function returns a pure 10-digit phone number if the number given is 10 digits or 11 digits starting with 1. If the number does not conform, the return value is false.

```php
<?php
function is_phone($phone) {
    $phone = preg_replace('/[^\d]+/', '', $phone);
    $num_digits = strlen($phone);
    if ($num_digits == 11 && $phone[0] == "1") {
        return substr($phone, 1);
    } else if ($num_digits == 10) {
        return $phone;
    } else {
        return false;
    }
}
?>
```

This script shows the power of regular expressions combined with standard string functions. The key is to first throw out any character that's not a digit—a perfect task for the preg_replace() function. Once you know that you have nothing but digits in a string, you can simply examine the string length to determine the number of digits, and the rest practically writes itself.

5

WORKING WITH TEXT AND HTML

Learning how to find, transform, and delete words is a critical skill for any webmaster. Some of the functions in this chapter are fairly simple, but I'll mention them just in case you haven't seen them. The more complex functions utilize *regular expressions*, a powerful part of PHP that every webmaster needs to know. Let's start with some of the more elementary string operations.

#34: Extracting Part of a String

For my day job, I sell collectible cards (think baseball cards with a fantasy twist). One of the interesting things about collectible cards is that people frequently search for cards in plural form—for example, *Shivan Dragons* instead of *Shivan Dragon.* This caused problems with our card lookup system because customer input of *Shivan Dragons* would not return any rows from a

MySQL query. To solve this problem, I used some string manipulation functions to examine the end of the user's query and remove instances of the letter *s*. Let's explore these functions in turn.

The substr() function allows you to extract part of a string for use in comparisons and other operations. For example, if the last letter in the string is an *s* character, you can chop it off and try again if the initial query produces no results.

The invocation of substr() is as follows:

```
substr(str, begin, end)
```

Here, *str* is the original string, *begin* is the starting character index, and *end* is the number of characters to remove. The start of a string is index 0. For example, the following code prints cde, the three characters starting at index 2:

```
echo substr('abcdef', 2, 3);
```

NOTE   *In order to calculate an index for substr(), you may need to know the length of your string. Use strlen(str) to determine a string's length.*

One very useful shortcut is that if you omit the *end* argument, substr() returns all of the characters from the starting index (*begin*) to the end of the string. Here's how to get all characters in a string starting at index 2:

```
echo substr('abcdef', 2);  // cdef
```

In addition, if you specify a negative value for *begin*, substr() (and many other string functions) starts counting from the end of the string, as in this example that extracts the next-to-last two characters of a string:

```
echo substr('abcdef', -3, 2);  // de
```

Once you find a substring that interests you, there are quite a number of things you can do to the string, including the following:

- **Reassign a specified portion of the string** by using substr() to chop off the excess characters. For example, $string = substr($string, 0, 10); sets $string to the first 10 characters of its original value.

- **Remove the final N characters** by using the substr() and strlen() functions together. For example, $string = substr($string, 0, strlen($string) - 3); sets $string to all but the last three characters of the initial value.

- **Replace characters** by using the substr_replace() function, which allows you to specify a substring and replace it with a string of your liking. For example, substr_replace('abcdef', 'bbb', 1, 2) returns abbbdef.

To see how you can use substrings in everyday programming, let's go back to the Shivan Dragons example. Recall that users might search for *Shivan Dragons*, but a single item may have a listing for *Shivan Dragon*. This code fragment shows one way to deal with this situation:

```
$sql = "SELECT * FROM product_table WHERE product_name = '$user_input'";
$result = @mysql_query($sql, $connection);

if (mysql_num_rows($result) == 0)  {
    // There were zero rows in the result set (no matching products).
    if (substr($user_input, -1) == 's') {
        // The last character in the string is an "s".
        $user_input = substr_replace($user_input, '', -1);
        // Remove last character in the string (the s).
        // Do another SQL query with the updated $user_input.
        $sql = "SELECT * FROM product_table WHERE product_name = '$user_input'";
        $result = @mysql_query($sql, $connection);
    }
}
```

This algorithm first checks the inventory against the string in $user_input. If there are no matches *and* the last character of $user_input is an *s*, it tries again without the *s*. Regardless of the last character, after running the algorithm you can examine the query result in $result.

Hacking the Script

One problem with this fragment is that you may have inventory under both *Shivan Dragons* and *Shivan Dragon*. As is, the script returns results for only one of these cases, and the search results are inconsistent, depending on the availability of the plural. For example, if you have one item listed as *Shivan Dragons* and two listed at *Shivan Dragon*, you'll get just the first item, but without the first item in the inventory, you'd get the other two.

You can add this functionality by using the substr() check to add to your SQL query instead of replacing it entirely. Here's how:

```
$sql = "SELECT * FROM product_table WHERE product_name = '$user_input'";
if (substr($user_input, -1) == 's') {
    // The last character in the string is an "s".
    // Add another possibility to the WHERE clause.
    $sql .= " OR product_name = '" . substr_replace($user_input, '', -1) . "'";
}
$result = @mysql_query($sql, $connection);
```

This is a considerably different approach, because it involves using a single SQL query to do all the work. Instead of trying a second query only when the first fails, the idea is to add another part to the OR clause in the query if the user input ends with an *s*.

#35: Making a String Uppercase, Lowercase, or Capitalized

One occasional problem with PHP is that MySQL supports case-insensitive character fields, but strings in PHP are case sensitive. In a query, MySQL makes no distinction between the words *Ferrett*, *FERRETT*, and *FerReTt*, but as strings in PHP, they have nothing in common. So in PHP you may need to change the case of characters in a string before you compare or print them.

PHP has three essential functions that convert string case: strtolower(), strtoupper(), and ucwords(). Here is a sample of them in action:

```
<?
$string = "heY hOw arE yoU doinG?";
echo strtoupper($string);
// Displays "HEY HOW ARE YOU DOING?"

echo strtolower($string);
// Displays "hey how are you doing?"

echo ucwords(strtolower($string));
// Displays "Hey How Are You Doing?"
?>
```

The functions work as follows:

- strtoupper() changes all of the characters in a string to uppercase.
- strtolower() changes all of the words in a string to lowercase.
- ucwords() converts the first letter of each word in a string to uppercase.

NOTE   *Notice that this script has a small trick; we used* strtolower() *before using* ucwords(). *Otherwise, the output would be HeY HOw ArE YoU DoinG?*

What Can Go Wrong?

There are a few hitches with ucwords(); the first is that it doesn't capitalize letters after a nonletter character, so a string like *mrs. johnston-brown* would become *Mrs. Johnston-brown* and *ac/dc* would be *Ac/dc*. If this bothers you, then you can create a function that uses regular expressions to explode the given string into an array of its individual words, then use ucwords() to capitalize each word, and finally join it back together into a single string.

A second concern is that ucwords() capitalizes certain words that *shouldn't* be capitalized, such as *and*, *or*, and *a*. If you want to use proper headline style, you can write a simple function that uses str_replace() to fix these words:

```
<?
function fussy_capitalize($string) {
    // Uppercase, but leave certain words in lowercase
    $uppercase_words = array("Of ","A ","The ","And ","An ", "Or ");
```

```php
    $lowercase_words = array("of ","a ","the ","and ","an ","or ");

    $string = ucwords(strtolower($string));
    $string = str_replace($uppercase_words, $lowercase_words, $string);
    // Uppercase the first word.
    return ucfirst($string);
}
?>
```

Finally, if you're working with names, ucwords(strtolower()) eradicates preexisting capitalizations, so a name such as *McMurdo* becomes *Mcmurdo*. If it's very important that you preserve these cases, but you still need to compare strings in PHP, use strcasecmp(*str1*, *str2*), which ignores case when comparing *str1* and *str2*.

#36: Finding Substrings

PHP has several functions that find a substring in a string. Your choice depends on what you want to do with the result. Here are three basic substring functions:

- strpos() finds the position of the substring's first occurrence.
- strrpos() finds the position of the last occurrence of the substring. Use this function in conjunction with substr() to extract everything past that point in the string.
- strstr() returns everything after the first occurrence of the substring.

All three of these functions return False if the substring isn't present. Because both a position and a string can evaluate to False when used in a conditional, it's very important that you check the type of the return value, as shown in the following script:

```php
<?php
$string = "I approve of Senator Foghorn's performance in the War on
Buttermilk. My name is Ferrett Steinmetz, and I approved this message.";
$search_term = "approve";
// Does it appear in the string?
$pos = strpos($string, 'approve');
if ($pos === False) {
    print "$term not in string\n";
} else {
    print "position: $pos\n";
    print "last position: " . strval(strrpos($string, $search_term)) . "\n";
    print strstr($string, $search_term) . "\n";
    // Prints "approve of Senator Foghorn's ... "
    print substr($string, strrpos($string, $search_term)) . "\n";
    // Prints "approved this message."
}
?>
```

What Can Go Wrong?

Three common problems can arise. First, you should always use the triple equals (===) instead of the double (==) in a comparison. The triple equals ensures that the values and the types of the terms are the same. This is important because you can get 0 as a valid position from strpos() and an empty string as a valid return value for strstr() and strrpos(), and both of these match False with ==.

Second, these functions are case sensitive. Using strstr($string, 'Approved') in the example above returns False. The case-insensitive versions of strpos(), strrpos(), and strstr() are stripos(), strripos, and stristr().

Finally, remember that this checks for very simple substrings, not *words*. If you need to do something fancy, such as finding words that start with *approv*, including *approval* and *approved* but not *disapprove*, you need something more powerful: regular expressions. We'll see how to use them in "#39: Regular Expressions" on page 69.

#37: Replacing Substrings

Use the str_replace() function to perform a simple string replacement. Here's how to replace *wabbit* with *duck* in a string taken from a cartoon:

```
$string = "It's wabbit season!";
print(str_replace("wabbit", "duck", $string));
```

Notice that str_replace() does not replace the substring in the original string. If you'd like to do that, reassign it to the original string:

```
$string = str_replace("wabbit", "duck", $string);
```

str_replace() has several extra features. To replace only the first *n* occurrences of a substring, add the number as a fourth parameter (this is especially handy for replacing just the first occurrence):

```
str_replace("wabbit", "duck", $string, n);
```

To delete all occurrences of a substring, just use an empty string as the replace argument:

```
$string = str_replace("wabbit", "", $string);
```

You can tell str_replace() to replace multiple substrings by placing them in an array:

```
$ugly_words = array("hamburger", "bacon", "bucket o'grease");
$string = str_replace($ugly_words, "Atkins-friendly foods", $string);
```

This example replaces all occurrences of *hamburger, bacon,* and *bucket o'grease* in $string with *Atkins-friendly foods.*

You can even provide two arrays of the same size as your search-and-replace arguments, and str_replace() replaces an item in the search array with the replacement item with the same index:

```
$ugly_words = array("hamburger", "bacon", "bucket o'grease");
$replacements = array("carrot", "broccoli", "2% milk");
$string = str_replace($ugly_words, $replacements, $string);
```

This replaces all instances of *hamburger* with *carrot*, all instances of *bacon* with *broccoli*, and all instances of *bucket o'grease* with *2% milk.*

What Can Go Wrong?

One problem with str_replace() is that it replaces *everything* that matches the pattern you gave it, no matter where it is in the string. If you replace *off* with *on*, you will discover that your *off*icials are now *on*icials and your c*off*ins are now c*on*ins.

Thus, while str_replace() is invaluable for stripping unwanted words from small-scale strings, you'll need regular expressions for more complex tasks. (See "#39: Regular Expressions" on page 69.)

#38: Finding and Fixing Misspelled Words with pspell

Anyone who's used Google has misspelled a word in a search, for example, *alternitive music.* And Google always helpfully comes back with *Did you mean alternative music?*

If you have a search function on your site, the ability to suggest misspelled words when no results (or not enough results) are found is an extremely helpful feature, especially since a customer's lack of spelling ability might cost you a sale. Fortunately, there's a PHP module called pspell, which allows you to check a word's spelling and suggest a replacement from pspell's default dictionary. If you like, you can even create a custom dictionary. To start with, though, you'll need to make sure that your PHP has the pspell library installed. Try this test script:

```
<?php
$dict_config = pspell_config_create('en', 'american');
?>
```

If you get an error, you don't have the pspell library installed. Flip back to "#18: Adding Extensions to PHP" on page 27 to see how to do this.

Working with the Default Dictionary

Here's a small function to get you started with pspell:

```php
<?php
function suggest_spelling($string) {
    // Suggest words for misspelled strings.
    $dict_config = pspell_config_create('en', 'american');
    pspell_config_ignore($dict_config, 3);
    pspell_config_mode($dict_config, PSPELL_FAST);
    $dictionary = pspell_new_config($dict_config);

    // Make sure we know whether we've suggested anything.
    $suggested_replacement = false;

    // Now we've got it set up, break it up by words.
    $string = explode(' ', $string);
    foreach ($string as $key=>$value) {
        $value = trim(str_replace(',', '', $value));
        if ( (strlen($value) > 3) && (! pspell_check($dictionary, $value)) ) {
            // If we can't find a suggestion
            $suggestion = pspell_suggest($dictionary, $value);
            // Suggestions are case sensitive, so check first
            if (strtolower($suggestion[0]) != strtolower($value)) {
                $string[$key] = $suggestion[0];
                $suggested_replacement = true;
            }
        }
    }

    if ($suggested_replacement) {
        // We had a suggestion, so return the data.
        return implode(' ', $string);
    } else {
        return null;
    }
}
?>
```

To use this function, call suggest_spelling() with a string argument, as in this example:

```php
<?
// Searchstring is taken from the previous form.
$searchstring = $_POST['customer_input'];

$spell_suggest = suggest_spelling($searchstring);
if ($spell_suggest) {
    // pspell found a suggestion.
    echo "Did you mean <i>$spell_suggest</i>?";
}
?>
```

To initialize pspell, you must configure a dictionary. To do so, you need to create a handle to a dictionary configuration file, modify a few settings on that handle, and then use the dictionary configuration to create a second handle to the actual dictionary.

If this sounds a little complicated, don't worry. The code rarely changes, so you can usually just copy it from another script. However, let's look at it piece by piece. Here is the code that configures the dictionary:

```
$dict_config = pspell_config_create('en', 'american');
pspell_config_ignore($dict_config, 3);
pspell_config_mode($dict_config, PSPELL_FAST);
```

$dict_config is the initial handle that controls the settings of your dictionary. You have to load all the settings into $dict_config and then create the dictionary with it. In this case, pspell_config_create() creates an English (en) dictionary with American spelling.

pspell_config_ignore() sets your dictionary to ignore all words of three letters and under. This is done because checking every *a* and *the* can be time consuming.

Finally, pspell_config_mode() tells pspell how you want to look things up. You have three choices:

- PSPELL_FAST is a quick method that returns as few suggested spellings as possible.
- PSPELL_NORMAL returns a medium number of spellings, at a normal rate.
- PSPELL_SLOW takes some time to check, but it returns the maximum possible number of suggestions.

We can use other configurations here (such as adding a custom dictionary, which I'll get to in a bit), but since this is a quick-and-dirty spell check, we'll just create the dictionary itself with this line:

```
$dictionary = pspell_new_config($dict_config);
```

There are two basic ways of using a dictionary at this point:

1. pspell_check($dictionary, *word*) returns True if *word* is in the dictionary.
2. pspell_suggest($dictionary, *word*) returns an array of suggested words if *word* isn't in the dictionary, with the first entry in the array being the most likely candidate. If the word is in the dictionary, or if there are no suggestions, this function returns nothing. The number of words that you get varies, but you get more with PSPELL_SLOW and fewer with PSPELL_FAST.

NOTE   *These functions do not check for contextual spellings.* Mary hat a ladle lam *checks out perfectly, even if you meant* Mary had a little lamb. *In addition, pspell always returns* True *if the word is under the string length set with* pspell_config_ignore(), *so in this case, a small but obviously misspelled word like* jlz *will still return* True.

Let's get back to the original script. Now that the dictionary is ready, we split the customer-submitted $string into an array of words, so *lemony snicket* becomes an array of *lemony* and *snicket*.

We then check each word against pspell's dictionary. Note that pspell doesn't like commas, so we remove the comma from the word before checking. If the word is longer than three characters, we check the spelling. If pspell detects a misspelling, we do the following:

1. We ask pspell to suggest an array of potential spellings for us.
2. We take the most likely spelling (the first item in the $suggestion array) and overwrite the old misspelled word with the new suggested word.
3. We set the $suggested_replacement flag to True to let us know at the end of the loop that we found a misspelled word somewhere in $string.

At the end of the loop, we check $suggested_replacement to see if there are any misspelled words. If so, we join the corrected words in $string with spaces and return that value. If there are no such words, we return null, indicating no misspellings.

Adding a Custom Dictionary to pspell

If a word isn't in the default dictionary, you can't easily add it. However, you can create a custom dictionary for use in conjunction with pspell's default dictionary. Here's how to do it:

Create a PHP-writable folder on your site and initialize the new dictionary there. Use the following script to create a new dictionary file custom.pws in the directory *path* on your server:

```
<?
$dict_config = pspell_config_create('en', 'american');
pspell_config_personal($dict_config, 'path/custom.pws');
pspell_config_ignore($dict_config, 2);
pspell_config_mode($dict_config, PSPELL_FAST);
$dictionary = pspell_new_config($dict_config);
?>
```

This is the script from the previous section but with one critical change: the addition of the pspell_config_personal() call that initializes a personal dictionary file. If no dictionary file is present, pspell creates an empty one for you.

You can add as many words as you like to your dictionary using this function:

```
pspell_add_to_personal($dictionary, word);
```

Words added to the dictionary are temporary unless you save them. Once you've finished adding words, add this line to the end of your script:

```
pspell_save_wordlist($dictionary);
```

Next, use the `pspell_config_personal()` call as above in any other script, and your new dictionary is ready for use alongside the default dictionary.

What Can Go Wrong?

Remember that pspell chokes on punctuation that isn't normally found in words—commas, semicolons, colons, and so on. You should strive to remove these from your words before adding them to your custom dictionary.

#39: Regular Expressions

Sooner or later, you'll have to roll up your sleeves and learn about regular expressions, which are the most powerful tools available for matching text. Want to find all the words within angle brackets in order to strip HTML code out of a string? You'll need regular expressions. Want to find any IP addresses in a string? Want to make sure a user-chosen password isn't just a sequence of numbers (like *123456*) or that it contains a mixture of uppercase and lower-case letters? Trying to sort through bad data in a database, and it turns out that your data entry people have listed a product's condition as *nearmint*, *near/mint*, *near mint*, and *near-mint*? You can use regular expressions to do all of these tasks.

However powerful regular expressions are, you should be aware that they can be difficult to read. For example, the following expression is cryptic unless you read it character by character:

```
/^(1[- ]*)?\(?\d{3}\)?[.- ]*\d{3}[.- ]*\d{4}$/
```

It looks like garbage at first, but this regular expression matches a phone number in a string. That's the trade-off of regexes; they do phenomenal things, but you have to build them character by character like the world's largest house of cards; mess up one character, and your entire pattern falls apart.

Let's go through the basics of regular expressions.

Regular Expression Basics

PHP has two kinds of regular expressions: POSIX Extended and Perl-Compatible. The POSIX Extended functions generally start with `ereg` and the Perl-Compatible with `preg`. There are minor syntax differences between the two and sometimes performance differences. The Perl-Compatible syntax is very popular, and we'll use those functions in this book.

One of the peculiarities of Perl-Compatible functions is that you need to enclose the expression within delimiter characters. Most developers use the slash (/) because it is similar to the way we search for regular expressions in the vi editor.

Let's say that you want to see if the word *fred* is in a string. The regular expression for that is just fred; it requires no special characters or modifiers. Here's how we'd put it to use with the preg_match() function:

```
if (preg_match('/fred/', 'I saw Alfred over there')) {
    print 'I found fred!';
}
```

Notice that the regular expression is a string, and the delimiter characters (the slashes) are inside the string. In addition, you should try to use the PHP single quotes instead of the double quotes, because PHP does not use variable expansion and escape sequences inside single-quoted strings. Regular expression syntax often clashes with escape sequences in double-quoted strings.

NOTE *A different delimiter such as the pipe (|) is handy when you have a slash-filled expression; for example, a URL.*

The delimiters in Perl-Compatible regular expressions are there mostly to make Perl people more comfortable and to confuse beginners, but they allow an extra set of features called *modifiers*, which you enable by placing extra characters after the second delimiter. The most common modifier is i, which makes the regular expression case insensitive. Therefore, if you wanted to search for *fred*, *Fred*, *FRED*, *fRed*, and so on, your regular expression would be /fred/i.

Special Character Sequences

To make regular expressions more compact and expand their utility, you can use a number of characters and sequences that match special circumstances. The most elementary (but still extremely useful) of these is the dot (.), which matches any character except a newline. So, for example, a regular expression of /f.ed/ matches *fled*, *fred*, *f!ed*, and so on. To match an actual dot (or anything else that is a special character) in a string, use a backslash; /f\.red/ matches only a string that contains *f.red*.

Here are a few other character sequences that come in handy:

- ^ matches the beginning of the string. For example, /^fred/ matches *fred* and *frederick* but not *alfred*.
- $ matches the end of the string. /fred$/ matches *fred* and *alfred* but not *frederick*.
- \s matches a whitespace character, such as a space or a tab.
- \S matches any non-whitespace character.
- \d matches any decimal digit (0–9).

You can find many others in the PHP manual, but these are the essentials.

Pattern Repeaters

Now it's time to start unlocking the real power of regular expressions by specifying how patterns can repeat. Let's start with the asterisk character (*), which means *match zero or more of whatever character or subexpression precedes the *.* For example, the expression /fr*ed/ matches *fed, fred, frred, frrred*, and so on. Combine this with the dot character and you have a DOS-style wildcard; /fr.*ed/ matches any string with an *fr* followed by any characters, and followed by *ed*; this includes *fred, fried, fritterpated*, and endless others.

The plus sign (+) repeater is similar, except that it means *one or more* instead of *zero or more*. Therefore, /fr.+ed/ does *not* match *fred*, but it matches anything else that /fr.*ed/ can.

The question mark (?) repeater means zero or one. For example, /photo-?synthesis/ matches *photosynthesis* and *photo-synthesis*.

Finally, you can specify a custom number of repetitions by using curly braces ({}). /fr.{3}ed/ matches anything containing *fr*, followed by three arbitrary characters, followed by *ed*. You can specify minimum and maximum occurrences as well; for example, {3,5} means *three to five instances*.

NOTE *Remember that you need to use a backslash if you want one of these characters literally! For example, to match fred?, use /fred\?/, not /fred?/.*

Grouping

The next regular expression trick we'll look at is how to group a series of characters in parentheses. The grouping simply means that you can use a repeater for a subexpression rather than a single character. For example, in the expression /f(re)+d/, the (re)+ means to match *re* one or more times. Therefore, the whole expression matches *fred, frered, frerered*, and so on.

Another feature that you often see inside groupings is the pipe (|) to tell PHP to match on either the left or the right side of the pipe. The expression /milk (and|or) meat/ matches both *milk and meat* and *milk or meat*. Another slightly more advanced example is /fred(ing|ed)?/, which matches *freding, freded*, and *fred*.

Character Classes

The final syntax that we'll explore is how to use square brackets ([]) to create a character class; that is, a set of characters that can pass as a single-character match. Use a dash to indicate a range of characters; for example, [0-9] matches any number of numeric characters, and [0-9a-fA-F] matches any hexadecimal character.

Using a caret (^) as the first character within a set of square brackets creates an inverted character class; that is, it will match everything except the characters in the brackets. For example, [^0-9] matches anything that's not 0 through 9.

Putting It All Together

You've now seen all of the essential building blocks of regular expressions. On their own, they don't do much, but when you put them together, you can create very powerful expressions. However, it's important to remember two things: first, it does take practice to learn how to create complex expressions, and second, you should always build even the most complicated expressions one step at a time. Let's walk through how the following regular expression works:

```
/<a\s+[^>]*href="[^"]+"/i
```

This regular expression matches an HTML anchor tag that has a link inside. Here's how the pieces break down:

1. All anchor tags start with `<a`, so this is the first piece.

2. Some whitespace must appear next, otherwise we'd match nonsense such as `<apple>`. Therefore, `\s+` appears next.

3. Now, we want to match any characters in the tag up to the link, because there might be some extra attributes such as `target="blank"` present. Tags ends with `>`, so we use `[^>]*` to match zero or more characters that aren't `>`. If this step doesn't sound very intuitive, you are correct. Typically, you'd realize the need for it (or, at least, only have the patience to deal with it) after writing the rest of the expression.

4. Link attributes start with `href="`, so we place that next. (For the sake of simplicity, for now we're ignoring the fact that some people leave out the quotes.)

5. Now we're at the first character of the link. We want to match the whole link. Therefore, we can use the same trick as in step 3; `[^"]+` matches one or more link characters.

6. To match the single quote that ends the attribute, we put in a double quotation mark (`"`). This might seem unnecessary because we've already matched the link, but it's usually best to follow up on our patterns just a little so that we don't accidentally match complete garbage.

7. The tag and attribute names in HTML are case insensitive, so we add the `i` modifier to the end of the expression after the delimiter.

As you can see, matching patterns with regular expressions is fairly simple. Now it's time to actually learn how to use them in PHP.

Matching and Extracting with Regular Expressions

PHP includes several regular expression functions. The easiest are the ones that tell you if there are any matches, what the matches are, and the locations of the matches. Let's start with the `preg_match()` function, which looks for a single match:

```php
<?php
$s = 'blah<a href="a.php">blah</a><a href="b.php">blah</a>';
if (preg_match('/<a\s+[^>]*href="[^"]+"/i', $s, $matches)) {
    print "match: $matches[0]";
}
?>
```

Here we're checking a string against the regular expression from the previous section. `preg_match()` takes at least two arguments: the expression and the search string. An additional `$matches` argument tells `preg_match()` to put the first matching substring inside a `$matches` array. In this case, only one element goes into this array, so we can access it at `$matches[0]`.

Continuing with this example, what if you want only the link in the match, not the characters that precede it? You can use grouping in your regular expression to demarcate the part you want to see:

```php
preg_match('/<a\s+[^>]*href="([^"]+)"/i', $s, $matches);
```

We indicate the grouping here with the parentheses around `[^"]+`. Now if there is a match, `$matches[0]` still contains the entire matching string, but `$matches[1]` contains the match inside the first grouping (in this case, a.php). If there were more groupings, they would be referenced with `$matches[2]`, `$matches[3]`, and so on.

At this point, it might be prudent to remind you of the `$print_r()` function, which prints the entire contents of an array. It can be really useful when you're trying to figure out how your match array works, especially if you want to find the character index of the matches as well, because the format of the match array *changes* if you want to know that information. To get that information, add a `PREG_OFFSET_CAPTURE` parameter:

```php
preg_match('/<a\s+[^>]*href="([^"]+)"/i', $s, $matches, PREG_OFFSET_CAPTURE);
```

Now if there's a match, `$matches[0]` and `$matches[1]` still contain the information for the entire match and the groupings, but instead of strings, they are arrays. The first element in one of these arrays is the match string; the second is the index of the match. Here's the slightly compressed output of `print_r($matches)` from our example:

```
Array (
    [0] => Array (
            [0] => <a href="a.php"
            [1] => 4
        )
```

```
    [1] => Array (
            [0] => a.php
            [1] => 13
        )
)
```

Extracting All Matches

To extract all of the matches of a regular expression, use `preg_match_all()`.
This function works just like `preg_match()`, but the match array has a different
structure, and the return value is the number of matches found. Let's say that
you use `$matches` as the match array again with the same example as the grouping in the previous section. Now `$matches[0]` corresponds to the first set of
matches—`$matches[0][0]` is the entire matching substring and `$matches[0][1]`
is the string match inside the grouping (a.php). And `$matches[1]` is an array
of the same structure that corresponds to the next match, so `$matches[1][1]` is
b.php in our example.

This can get really ugly, especially if you add a `PREG_OFFSET_CAPTURE`
parameter, because that parameter replaces all of the strings in the match
array with another layer of arrays, just as it did with `preg_match()`. Again,
remember `print_r()`; it can be invaluable here.

Replacing Substrings with Regular Expressions

The `preg_replace()` function works much like `preg_match()`, but it also replaces
matched substrings and returns the result. Let's start with a simple example,
where we want to see what happens if we use *deb* to replace any occurrence
matching `/fre+d/` in `$s`:

```
print preg_replace('/fre+d/', 'deb', $s);
```

This is great, but there's more power to unlock. Let's say that you want to
use part of the original string—instead of just *deb*, you want to keep the *es*
from the original string. In this case, *fred* becomes *deb*, *freed* becomes *deeb*, and
so on. To do this, group the relevant part of the regular expression, and then
use a *backreference* in the replacement. Here's how to do it in this example:

```
print preg_replace('/fr(e+)d/', 'd$1b', $s);
```

The grouping is done with parentheses as before, and the backreference
is the `$1` in the replacement, meaning *the first group*. If you have more than
one group, use `$2`, `$3`, and so on to reference them. The entire match is in `$0`.

NOTE   *You may see backreferences with a backslash (\0, \1, \2, and so on). This is older syntax with the same meaning.*

#40: Rearranging a Table

Let's look at several utilities that use regular expressions. For a more complex example, let's say that you have a bunch of entries in an HTML table that looks like this:

```
<tr><td>last_name, first_name</td>
<td>address</td>
<td>phone number</td>
</tr>
```

Now assume that your boss just can't leave well enough alone and insists that you change it to this format:

```
<tr><td>first_name</td>
<td>last_name</td>
<td>address</td>
<td>phone number</td>
</tr>
```

You can do this in one fell swoop with backreferencing:

```
$table = preg_replace('/<td>([^<]*),\s*([^<]*)<\/td>/',
                       '<td>$1</td>' . "\n" . '<td>$2</td>',
                       $table);
```

A bit of explanation is necessary. I split the arguments into three lines because they're easier to read that way. Notice that there are two groupings, and before the second (the last name), there is a \s* to match any excess whitespace. Finally, notice how the replacement is a concatenation. That's because we want a newline, but \n represents a newline only in double-quoted strings. Otherwise, you want to use single-quoted strings, or else you may need to add a bunch of backslashes in your backreferences.

Now just make sure to tell your boss that this task took you forever, so that you still have time to play video games while pretending to work.

#41: Creating a Screen Scraper

A *screen scraper* program accesses a web page and picks through the HTML for interesting or useful data. Here's a very simple one that extracts all hyperlinks from a page and then categorizes them. This scraper includes a lot of regular expressions, so let's take it one step at a time. First, let's check that the input (in $_REQUEST["page"]) is actually a hyperlink and not someone trying to monkey around with files on the local system:

```
<?php
$page = $_REQUEST["page"];
if (!preg_match('|^https{0,1}://|', $page)) {
    print "URL $page invalid or unsupported.";
    exit;
}
```

Let's say that this checks out, so now it's time to get the data and extract all of the hyperlinks in the anchor tags (see the example on page 72). Notice that we're using the simple file_get_contents() function instead of cURL; this assumes that we don't need any of cURL's fancy features such as HTTP authentication or cookie management.

```
$data = file_get_contents($page);
preg_match_all('|<a\s[^>]*href="([^"]+)"|i', $data, $matches);
```

Now all of the hyperlinks are in $matches[1] (remember that $matches[0] contains all the matches). Let's initialize some arrays that we'll use to store and categorize the hyperlinks:

```
$all_links = array();
$js_links = array();
$full_links = array();
$local_links = array();
```

It's time to run through all of the links and do the real work of categorization. First, we make sure that we haven't already seen this link. If it's a new one, we'll use several regular expressions to determine what kind of link it is:

```
foreach ($matches[1] as $link) {
    if ($all_links[$link]) {
        continue;
    }
    $all_links[$link] = true;

    if (preg_match('/^javascript:/', $link)) {
        $js_links[] = $link;
    } elseif (preg_match('/^https{0,1}:/i', $link)) {
        $full_links[] = $link;
    } else {
        $local_links[] = $link;
    }
}
```

Now it's time to print the results of the analysis (shown in Figure 5-1):

```
print '<table border="0">';
print "<tr><td>number of links:</td><td>";
print strval(count($matches[1])) . "</td></tr>";
print "<tr><td>unique links:</td><td>";
print strval(count($all_links)) . "</td></tr>";
print "<tr><td>local links:</td><td>";
print strval(count($local_links)) . "</td></tr>";
print "<tr><td>full links:</td><td>";
print strval(count($full_links)) . "</td></tr>";
print "<tr><td>javascript junk:</td><td>";
print strval(count($js_links)) . "</td></tr>";
print '</table>';
?>
```

```
number of links: 210
unique links:    141
local links:      89
full links:       36
javascript junk:  16
```

Figure 5-1: The anchor tag summary

Hacking the Script

You can go crazy with a script like this: categorize to your heart's content, follow a few links, or whatever. However, one very useful exercise is figuring out how to break the original URL into its component pieces so that you can make local (relative) links into full URLs.

#42: Converting Plaintext into HTML-Ready Markup

One annoying web aspect of programming is that HTML and plaintext aren't compatible, yet they are frequently used interchangeably. People type things into text areas of forms in plaintext, but chances are pretty good you want to display them in HTML.

Here's an example of something that you might find on a form:

Hey folks,

I recently had my brain removed as a part of my therapy. I am fine, and I can now enjoy Pauly Shore movies with my friends.

Sincerely,

Fred

Because there are no <BR /> or <P> tags in the markup for line breaks, it looks like this when pumped back into a web browser as HTML:

Hey folks, I recently had my brain removed as a part of my therapy. I am fine, and I can now enjoy Pauly Shore movies with my friends. Sincerely, Fred

Although blindly echoing whatever text the user gives you is a bad idea because you leave yourself open to XSS attacks, let's ignore that for now (you can read more about how to get rid of this stuff in "#20: Preventing Basic XSS Attacks" on page 37) and assume that you trust the user.

The simplest way to convert the newlines to HTML is with the nl2br() PHP function. Unfortunately, this method is rather inflexible because it translates every newline into a <br> tag. If you have HTML mixed in with the plaintext, it can start to look ugly. Take this sample HTML:

```
<table>
<tr><td>Hi, I'm a row in a table
</td></tr>
</table>
```

nl2br() transforms this HTML into the following:

```
<table><br>
<tr><td>Hi, I'm a row in a table<br>
</td></tr><br>
</table><br>
```

This code has a far different rendering than the original. During my search for a better replacement, I came across a great script from Matthew Mullenweg, the founding developer of WordPress. It's called autop():

```
<?
function autop($pee, $br = 1) {
// Converts plaintext to HTML-compliant stuff

    $pee = $pee . "\n"; // Just to make things a little easier, pad the end.
    $pee = preg_replace('|<br />\s*<br />|', "\n\n", $pee);
    $pee = preg_replace('!(<(?:table|ul|ol|li|pre|form|blockquote|h[1-
6])[^>]*>)!', "\n$1", $pee); // Space things out a little.
    $pee = preg_replace('!(</(?:table|ul|ol|li|pre|form|blockquote|h[1-
6])>)!', "$1\n", $pee); // Space things out a little.
    $pee = preg_replace("/(\r\n|\r)/", "\n", $pee); // Cross-platform newlines.
    $pee = preg_replace("/\n\n+/", "\n\n", $pee); // Take care of duplicates.
    $pee = preg_replace('/\n?(.+?)(?:\n\s*\n|\z)/s', "\t<p>$1</p>\n", $pee);
    // Make paragraphs, including one at the end.
    $pee = preg_replace('|<p>\s*?</p>|', '', $pee); // Under certain strange
conditions, it could create a P of entirely whitespace.
    $pee = preg_replace("|<p>(<li.+?)</p>|", "$1", $pee); // Problem with
nested lists
    $pee = preg_replace('|<p><blockquote([^>]*)>|i', "<blockquote$1><p>",
$pee);
    $pee = str_replace('</blockquote></p>', '</p></blockquote>', $pee);
    $pee = preg_replace('!<p>\s*(</?(?:table|tr|td|th|div|ul|ol|li|pre|select|
form|blockquote|p|h[1-6])[^>]*>)!', "$1", $pee);
    $pee = preg_replace('!(</?(?:table|tr|td|th|div|ul|ol|li|pre|select|form|
blockquote|p|h[1-6])[^>]*>)\s*</p>!', "$1", $pee);
    if ($br) $pee = preg_replace('|(?<!<br />)\s*\n|', "<br />\n", $pee); //
Optionally make line breaks.
    $pee = preg_replace('!(</?(?:table|tr|td|th|div|dl|dd|dt|ul|ol|li|pre|
select|form|blockquote|p|h[1-6])[^>]*>)\s*<br />!', "$1", $pee);
    $pee = preg_replace('!<br />(\s*</?(?:p|li|div|th|pre|td|ul|ol)>)!', '$1',
$pee);
    $pee = preg_replace('/&([^#])(?![a-z]{1,8};)/', '&#038;$1', $pee);

    return $pee;
}
?>
```

Run autop() with a single argument: the string you want to filter. The return value is the filtered string. autop() is smart enough to preserve block-level HTML elements (tables and formatted lists won't have additional

`<br />`s inserted randomly wherever there's whitespace) while ignoring existing `<P>`s and `<br />`s. Consider the following code:

```
print autop('A haiku is five                <br />

Syllables on other lines
Seven in the middle    ');
```

Running this fragment results in this output:

```
<p>A haiku is five              </p>
<p>Syllables on other lines<br />
Seven in the middle
</p>
```

The autop() function has three basic phases: cleanup, replacement, and tag stripping. Before detailing each phase, we need to look at the grouping modifiers found throughout the function. In particular, what does (?:*stuff*) mean in a regular expression?

It's a grouping that is identical to (*stuff*), but the ?: tells the regular expression parser not to backreference this grouping. That is, you want to know about the value inside the parentheses, but you want to use features of grouping—pattern repetition on a grouping, options, and so on. This makes it a lot easier to keep track of the groupings that you actually *do* care about, especially if you have to insert a grouping after you've written a lot of code that depends on a certain backreference. Consider this expression from the autop() code:

```
!(</(?:table|ul|ol|li|pre|form|blockquote|h[1-6])>)!
```

This means *find any tag with either table, ul, ol, li, pre, form, blockquote, or h1 through h6*. But all Matthew Mullenweg cares about here is the grouping; it allows him to specify many tags in a single regular expression.

Without getting into a line-by-line script analysis, the workflow of autop() is as follows:

1. **Cleanup.** The autop() script replaces all instances of multiple `<br>`s with newlines, changes any cross-platform newlines to work on Unix (Unix uses a simple \n, while Windows uses \r\n), and reduces any arbitrarily large strings of newlines down to a pair of lines.

2. **Replacement.** autop() finds any newline, followed by text, followed by two newlines and replaces the newlines with proper paragraph tags, as in `<p>Stuff</p>`.

3. **Tag-stripping.** autop() looks for any block-level HTML elements (such as numbered lists and tables) that a `<p>` or `<br>` would screw up and removes those `<p>` and `<br>` tags.

#43: Automatically Hyperlinking URLs

Most forum and blog software automatically convert URLs in posts and comments into hyperlinked text. You could probably think of a simple way to implement this feature in your own site by matching *http://* and then using a backreference to add an anchor tag around it. However, what if someone is actually using an anchor tag? Then you'd get a real mess!

Therefore, you need to think of a way to make sure that the URL is not already inside an anchor tag. You might think of using the grouping modifier ?!, which says *reject anything that matches this group*. However, this works in a regular expression only if the unwanted group follows what you want to match, because of the way regular expressions work—they consume input one character at a time and never look back. Therefore, you need a feature called a *lookbehind assertion* that essentially states *check this condition when you get a match later on in the regular expression*. To denote a negative lookbehind assertion, use a ?<! grouping modifier.

This said, here's the code for autolinking URLs, where we don't want to disturb anything that is prefixed by the href=" that you'd find in an anchor tag:

```
preg_replace('|(?<!href=")(https?://[A-Za-z0-9+\-=._/*(),@\'$:;&!?%]+)|i',
             '<a href="$1">$1</a>',
             $string);
```

Most of this regular expression is a character class containing the valid characters in a URL. Obviously, there are numerous variations on this theme—checking for valid domains, looking for exceptions on other weird HTML, looking for a trailing dot or comma, and so on. You probably needn't get too carried away.

#44: Stripping HTML Tags from Strings

Regular expressions are useful, but they're not the solution to every problem. Let's say that you plan to display possibly HTML-rich text inside another HTML page, and you need to strip out any possibly harmful HTML. Use the strip_tags() function:

```
<?php
print strip_tags($string);
?>
```

To add a few tags that you think users should be able to use, add an extra string parameter containing the open tags that you want to permit:

```
print strip_tags($string, "<i><b><p>");
```

This function is just one of many text-processing functions that PHP offers as an alternative to regular expressions or other do-it-yourself solutions. It's always worth a trip to the PHP manual to see if there's a built-in for your needs. But don't be afraid to get your hands dirty when necessary.

6

WORKING WITH DATES

This chapter shows you how to work with dates and times with PHP. Web programs often involve an extensive amount of extraction, manipulation, comparison, and display of dates. The task gets more involved when you add MySQL to the mix. But first, let's talk about the native time format on your server.

How Unix Time Works

Before going into detail about how to work magic with dates, I have to get into the basics of how POSIX-compliant Unix/Linux servers (and thus, PHP) keep time. Fortunately, it's a fairly simple system.

Midnight, January 1, 1970, is when time "began" for Unix computers. In Unix parlance, that timestamp is 0, and it's called the *epoch date*.

Any date since then is calculated as the number of seconds that have elapsed between January 1, 1970, and that time. For example, as I write this at 12:17:25 PM on January 11, 2008, 1,200,082,645 seconds have passed since that fabled date. Thus, the timestamp as I write this is—you guessed it—1200082645.

This scheme makes manipulating dates in PHP relatively easy as long as you don't need to show the date in a readable format. For example, you can jump ahead a day by adding (60 × 60 × 24) seconds to the current timestamp or go back one hour by subtracting 3,600 seconds. Table 6-1 is a handy chart to reference when working with timestamps.

Table 6-1: Common Time Increments as Measured in Seconds

Seconds	Time
60	One minute
3,600	One hour
28,800	Eight hours
86,400	One day
604,800	One week

Because the timestamp is just a number, you can easily compare two timestamps. If one timestamp is greater than a second timestamp, then the first timestamp corresponds to the later date of the two. This is particularly handy when you compare against the current timestamp.

In addition to extracting, manipulating, and storing timestamps, this chapter shows you how to convert them to readable dates and get other details, such as the day of the week. In addition, we'll touch on how to work with date formats in MySQL.

#45: Getting the Current Timestamp

To get the current timestamp, call the time() function with no arguments. The return value is the current timestamp on the server. This simple example prints the current time:

```
echo 'The current timestamp is ' . time();
```

You can also assign the returned value of the time() function to variables, like so:

```
$time = time();
```

Many PHP date-related functions take a timestamp argument, and most of them use the current time if you don't supply that parameter. For example, the date() function returns a formatted date string in a custom format (like *Nov 1, 2006*), by using the syntax date("*format*", *timestamp*). But if you don't give it a timestamp, the default is the current time. This means that for most of the time functions, you don't even need to include time() as a parameter if you want to work with the current timestamp.

NOTE   *A timestamp is always expressed as UTC (Coordinated Universal Time, a very precise worldwide time standard). However, date/time display functions use your server's time zone to figure out the local time to display. For example, a timestamp of 1136116800 would be 1:00 AM on a Middle European Time (MET) server, but 7:00 PM the previous day on a server set using Eastern Standard Time.*

#46: Getting the Timestamp of a Date in the Past or Future

Now that you know how to get the current timestamp, let's explore how to determine some other timestamps close to the current time. For example, you can extract yesterday's timestamp or, say, next Friday's. There are two general methods for finding these values:

- Determining the timestamp based on a string
- Determining the timestamp from date values (which can be a bit trickier)

Creating Timestamps from a String

The strtotime() function can sometimes be a PHP programmer's best friend. Just as its name suggests, strtotime() generates a timestamp from an English date-phrase, such as *April 1* or *Friday*. These strings can be either relative to the current date or absolute. Table 6-2 outlines some of the possibilities.

Table 6-2: strtotime() Examples

Invocation	Output (as a timestamp)
strtotime("Friday")	Friday at midnight
strtotime("+1 week Friday")	The Friday after next at midnight
strtotime("+1 week")	A week from right now
strtotime("-2 months")	Two months ago from right now
strtotime("October 1, 2008")	October 1, 2008, at midnight
strtotime("2008-10-01")	October 1, 2008, at midnight
strtotime("Friday 12:01 p.m.")	Friday at 12:01 PM
strtotime("+7 days 12:01 p.m.")	Seven days from now at 12:01 PM

Although most date formats work with strtotime(), some cause strtotime() to choke—and it's not always obvious which ones work and which ones don't. For example, strtotime("2008-10-01") works fine, but strtotime("10-01-2008") produces a weird time that translates to June 28, 2015. For consistent results, use full ISO 8601–compliant dates (see http://www.cl.cam.ac.uk/~mgk25/iso-time.html), which take the form of *YYYY-MM-DD*. This format is particularly important because it is one of several that MySQL understands, as you will see in "MySQL Date Formats" on page 90.

If strtotime() can't translate your request at all, it will return either false (on PHP version 5.1 or later) or -1 (on earlier versions of PHP). The -1 result in particular can be troubling, since it means that strtotime()'s failures will often be read by the date-processing functions as *December 31, 1969*, also known as *one second before the epoch date*.

Verifying Dates with strtotime()

You can sometimes use strtotime() to verify that a date is within a valid date range. For example, if you're allowing the user to input a date in the form of *2008-01-01*, you can verify that the date input is correct by using strtotime(). Of course, whether the date is *valid* is another thing. A user could input *yesterday* and it would pass as true. If you're putting a date into a database, for instance, you should use an additional layer of date checking to ensure that you get a valid field. The following script checks a user-supplied date to see if it falls in a valid range and then transforms it into a date format for your database:

```php
<?php
$user_supplied_date = $_GET['date'];
$user_timestamp = strtotime($user_supplied_date);

// Beginning/end of valid date range
$start_date = strtotime('2008-01-01');
$end_date = strtotime('2009-01-01');


if ($user_timestamp < $start_date ||
    $user_timestamp >= $end_date) {
    die('Date does not fall within the valid range of dates');
}

$database_date = date('Y-m-d', $user_timestamp);
// Now use $database_date in a database query.

?>
```

NOTE   *You'll see how to use the date() formatting function later in this chapter.*

Creating Timestamps from Date Values

If you know the precise date and time you need, you can create a timestamp with the mktime() function. To use the mktime() function, you need the hour, the minute, the second, the number of the month, the day, and the year of the timestamp you want to create.

For example:

```php
$future_date = mktime($hour, $minute, $second, $month, $day, $year);
```

You can omit arguments from the right; in this case, `mktime()` uses the values from the current time. For example, `mktime(12, 00, 0)` creates a timestamp value of noon on the month, day, and year of today. You have to pass `mktime()` actual numbers, not strings with numbers in them. It may seem annoying, but `mktime('12', '05', '2008')` causes errors.

NOTE   *If you're creating a date with `mktime()`, it's generally best to set a default hour of 12, just in case your server has an issue with time zones. For example, some servers are set to use UTC, but if PHP is set to use Eastern Standard Time, creating a timestamp for a date starting at midnight might not register as that date for another four hours.*

A common programmer's trick is to use the `date()` (see "#47: Formatting Dates and Times" below) and `strtotime()` functions to get the current month or day for use in a `mktime()` statement.

For example, this line of code uses the `date()` function to get the current month in 01-12 number format and then inserts it into the month position of the `mktime()` function:

```
$first_of_this_month = mktime(0, 0, 0, intval(date("m")), 1);
```

And this snippet of code uses the `strtotime()` function to get the next month in timestamp format and then converts that timestamp into both a 01–12 month number and a four-digit year for use in the `mktime()` function. (Note that we specifically use the year here in case of a December-to-January annual rollover, where December 15's next month would also be next year.)

```
$next_month_timestamp = strtotime("+1 month");
$first_of_next_month = mktime(0, 0, 0, intval(date("m",
$next_month_timestamp)), 1, intval(date("y", $next_month_timestamp)));
```

Of course, the `mktime()` function isn't enough sometimes, because we not only work with months and days, we work with weeks. That's when we want `strtotime()`.

One final function that works well in conjunction with `mktime()` is `checkdate()`, which checks a month, a day, and year for a valid date. The return value of `true` or `false` indicates whether this is a date that exists on the calendar. For example, `checkdate(12, 31, 2008)` returns `true`, whereas `checkdate(2, 31, 2008)` returns `false`.

Now that you've seen how to create and manipulate dates in PHP, let's look at how to print them out.

#47: Formatting Dates and Times

Because humans don't understand timestamps very well, whenever you want to print a date, you should use a format such as *Oct 15, 2008.*

We already touched on the `date()` function earlier in this chapter; now let's look at how it works. Its two parameters are a date format (such as `'M j, Y'`) and a timestamp, and the return value is a string. For example, date('M j, Y', 1151884800) yields *Jul 2, 2006* in Pacific Standard Time. If you omit the timestamp parameter, date() uses the current time.

The date format can have extra characters, such as colons and commas, but unlike other functions that take a format—such as printf()—you must be especially careful not to use reserved formatting characters because there is no format prefix. Table 6-3, cheerfully ripped straight from the official PHP documents, outlines the format strings.

Table 6-3: date() Format Strings

Date Format Character	Description	Example Returned Values
Day		
d	Day of the month, two digits with leading zeros	01 to 31
D	A textual representation of a day, three letters	Mon through Sun
j	Day of the month without leading zeros	1 to 31
l (lowercase L)	A full textual representation of the day of the week	Sunday through Saturday
S	English ordinal suffix for the day of the month, two characters	st, nd, rd, or th; works well with j
w	Numeric representation of the day of the week	0 (for Sunday) through 6 (for Saturday)
z	The day of the year	0 through 365
Week		
W	ISO-8601 week number of year, weeks starting on Monday (added in PHP 4.1.0)	42 (the 42nd week in the year)
Month		
F	A full textual representation of a month, such as January or March	January through December
m	Numeric representation of a month, with leading zeros	01 through 12
M	A short textual representation of a month, three letters	Jan through Dec
N	Numeric representation of a month, without leading zeros	1 through 12
t	Number of days in the given month	28 through 31

Table 6-3: date( ) Format Strings (continued)

Date Format Character	Description	Example Returned Values
Year		
L	Represents a leap year	1 if it is a leap year, 0 otherwise
Y	A full numeric representation of a year, four digits	1999 or 2003
y	A two-digit representation of a year	99 or 03
Time		
a	Lowercase ante meridiem and post meridiem	am or pm
A	Uppercase ante meridiem and post meridiem	AM or PM
B	Swatch Internet time	000 through 999
g	12-hour format of an hour without leading zeros	1 through 12
G	24-hour format of an hour without leading zeros	0 through 23
h	12-hour format of an hour with leading zeros	01 through 12
H	24-hour format of an hour with leading zeros	00 through 23
i	Minutes, with leading zeros	00 through 59
s	Seconds, with leading zeros	00 through 59
Time Zone		
I	Represents daylight saving time	1 if daylight saving time, 0 otherwise
O	Difference from UST in hours	+0200
T	Time zone setting of this machine	EST, MDT, etc.
Z	Time zone offset in seconds. The offset for time zones west of UTC is always negative, and is always positive for time zones east of UTC.	-43200 through 43200
Full Date/Time		
c	ISO 8601 date (added in PHP 5)	2008-12-18T16:01:07 +02:00
r	RFC 2822 formatted date	Thu, 18 Dec 2008 16:01:07 +0200

Unrecognized characters in the format string are to be printed as-is. If you want to use reserved characters as literals, you can escape them with a backslash, as in date("l \\t\h\e jS"). Unfortunately, it's very easy to lose track of the number of backslashes you may need, because backslashes are used in certain string escape sequences.

Table 6-4 contains some example date formats.

Table 6-4: date() Function Sample Strings

Date Format String	Sample Output
l (lowercase L)	Saturday
M	Oct
H:m	1:36
G:i:s A	5:26:01 PM
m-d-Y	10-04-2008
M-j-y	Jun-1-08
M-d-Y h:m:s a	Aug-16-2008 12:08:00 am

#48: Calculating the Day of the Week from a Given Date

As a derivation of "#47: Formatting Dates and Times" on page 85, let's look at how to get very specific information from a date.

Once again, getting the timestamp of a date is the key to everything:

```php
<?php
$timestamp = strtotime("2008-07-03");
$day_of_week = date('l', $timestamp);
echo 'The day of the week is ' . $day_of_week;
?>
```

This script performs three simple steps:

1. Stores the timestamp for July 3, 2008 in $timestamp.
2. Uses the date() format function to extract the day of week for $timestamp.
3. Prints the day of the week.

#49: Finding the Difference Between Two Dates

If you find yourself in a situation where you need to know how much time has elapsed between a pair of dates, here's what you're looking for.

```php
<?php

function calculate_time_difference($timestamp1, $timestamp2, $time_unit) {
    // Determines difference between two timestamps

    $timestamp1 = intval($timestamp1);
    $timestamp2 = intval($timestamp2);
    if ($timestamp1 && $timestamp2) {
        $time_lapse = $timestamp2 - $timestamp1;

        $seconds_in_unit = array(
```

```php
            'second'    => 1,
            'minute'    => 60,
            'hour'      => 3600,
            'day'       => 86400,
            'week'      => 604800,
        );

        if ($seconds_in_unit[$time_unit]) {
            return floor($time_lapse/$seconds_in_unit[$time_unit]);
        }
    }

    return false;
}
?>
```

The `calculate_time_difference()` function takes three arguments: the first timestamp, the second timestamp, and the measurement in which you want the difference. That measurement can be second, hour, day, or week.

The script first forces the timestamps into numerical form and then subtracts the second timestamp value from the first to determine the total number of seconds between the two measurements. (Remember, timestamps are merely the number of seconds that have elapsed since the epoch date of January 1, 1970, so the difference between any two timestamps is in seconds.) Next, it checks an array to see what measurement unit the user wants the data returned in. The units are measured in seconds. If it's a valid unit, the function divides the total number of elapsed seconds by the number of seconds in the chosen unit. For example, if the user has chosen *minute* and the difference between the two timestamps is 60, then 60 seconds elapsed divided by 60 seconds in a minute equals 1 minute.

If the user chooses an invalid unit (or inputs incorrect timestamps), the function returns false as a default.

Using the Script

This example translates a time difference of seven days into all of the units.

```php
<?php
// Get the current time and seven days from now as an example.
$timestamp_1 = time();
$timestamp_2 = strtotime('+7 days');

$units = array("second", "minute", "hour", "day", "week");
foreach ($units as $u) {
    $nunits = calculate_time_difference($timestamp_1, $timestamp_2, $u);

    echo $nunits . " $u(s) have passed between " . date("m-d-Y", $timestamp_1)
. ' and ' . date("m-d-Y", $timestamp_2);
    print "\n";
}
?>
```

Hacking the Script

This script can return negative values if the second timestamp comes before the first. For example, if $timestamp_1 is from July 7, 2008, and $timestamp_2 is July 1, 2008, the difference is returned as 6 days. If all you care about is the total difference, then put in this bit of code to replace the $time_lapse = $timestamp_2 - $timestamp1 segment:

```
if ($timestamp2 > $timestamp1) {
    $time_lapse = abs($timestamp2 - $timestamp1);
}
```

This will always return a positive value (or, at worst, zero), no matter what order the dates are in.

Now that we've seen the details of PHP dates and times, let's finish with a short discussion of MySQL dates and times.

MySQL Date Formats

Much like PHP, MySQL 5 uses a form of timestamp, but in its native form, it is not compatible with the PHP timestamp. MySQL has three time/date field types: DATE (a date), TIME (a time), and DATETIME (a date and a time). MySQL also has a special date field type called TIMESTAMP, which works like DATETIME but automatically updates to the current timestamp with every insert and update and has a different internal storage mechanism.

There are numerical ways of representing data in your queries for these types, but it's much easier to use a string in your SQL. For example, you can use *2008-09-26* as a date, *13:23:56* as a time, and *2008-09-26 13:23:56* as a date and time. To convert a PHP timestamp in $timestamp into a form suitable for MySQL, use this code:

```
date('Y-m-d H:i:s', $timestamp)
```

Although you can store PHP/Unix timestamps as INT(10), it really helps to use the native MySQL formats, because you will be able to use the data independently of PHP. To get a PHP timestamp from a SELECT query, use the SQL UNIX_TIMESTAMP() function, as in this skeleton example:

```
SELECT UNIX_TIMESTAMP(my_date) FROM table;
```

MySQL 5 has a lot of very useful date functions, such as DATE_FORMAT and DATE_ADD. For a complete list, check out the online documentation at http://www.mysql.com/.

7

WORKING WITH FILES

File manipulation is an important part of PHP programming. To accomplish your task, you may need to create text files on the fly, read tab-delimited files to import huge chunks of data, or perhaps even create cache files for speeding up your server and reducing processor overhead.

File Permissions

In order to do any useful file operations, PHP needs permission to access files. On most webservers, PHP can read files easily enough, but it does not have the necessary permissions to create and alter files. This is a *good* thing, because universal file write access usually gives hackers carte blanche to do whatever they like with your server.

On Unix servers, there are three sets of permissions for owner, group, and world. The user ID that owns the file is the *owner*, and every user on the system is *world* (we won't discuss *group* in this book; set the group permissions to the permissions of world).

Secure servers treat PHP as a very unprivileged user that does not have write access to anything on the system. You don't want PHP to have any rights on the machine because external users influence at least part of what PHP does. If they find some way to compromise PHP, you don't want that to carry over to the rest of your system.

There are three basic ways to access a file, so there are three kinds of file permissions: read, write, and execute. They're independent, so, for example, you can grant read and execute permission without granting write access.

- *Read* allows PHP to read a file, that is, examine its contents. For directories, read access gives permission to see the contents of the directory (but not necessarily access the contents; see *Execute* below).

- *Write* allows PHP to change the contents of the file, remove the file (delete it), and (in a directory) create a new file or subdirectory.

- *Execute* allows PHP to run programs. This is usually a bad idea, since it allows the server to run malicious programs. If you've set your server up properly for the Web, PHP scripts should run just fine without execute permission. Execute permission has a different meaning in directories; it allows for access to the files inside the directory (assuming you have read access to those files). Therefore, you often need to set execute permissions in conjunction with read access on directories.

Most files are set to *read* by default for user, group, and world permission sets. In addition, the user normally has write access. Directories are the same, except they nearly always have *execute* permission set when the read permission is set.

If you want PHP to create new files (and you need to do so for several scripts in this book), you need to create a directory where PHP has write access.

The most common way to set permissions is an absolute one, where you set the user, group, and world at once with a three-digit numeric code. For example, the code for *user read/write, group read, world read* is *644*, with *6* for *user*, *4* for *group*, and *4* for *world*. Each digit is a bitfield. The most practical values are as follows:

0: no permissions

4: read permissions

5: read/execute permissions

6: read/write permissions

7: read/write/execute permissions

There are two primary ways to set permissions: with an FTP program and on the command line. Let's look at both.

Permissions with an FTP Program

Most FTP programs allow you to set permissions for files and directories. You can usually right-click the directory and look for an option such as CHMOD,

Set Permissions, or Properties. A dialog box should appear. If all else fails, of course, read the documentation that comes with the FTP program.

For a directory, you should normally set the permissions to 755 (as shown below), which is Unix code for *owner read/write/execute, group read/execute, world read/execute*. Set the properties, and click **OK**. For files, the mode should be 644, which is the same except without the execute bits.

The Command Line

If you have access to a Unix shell prompt, you can use a much more direct method to change the permissions of a directory so that the owner can write and everyone else can read and execute. Just type the following:

```
chmod 755 directory
```

What Can Go Wrong?

Among the several problems that could occur is that your ISP could be running PHP as a different user than your login. In this case, you may need to set world write permissions, and your ISP may automatically detect and disallow this. If so, you'll just have to settle for read access to files, and there's plenty you can do with just that.

Keep in mind that giving write access to a directory potentially opens you to a number of security problems. You should never let PHP run any files in a writeable directory—in fact, you should keep that directory off-limits to the webserver. If you're not careful about how your scripts name and access files, you could be in for a heap of trouble.

#50: Placing a File's Contents into a Variable

Let's say that you want to put all of the content of a text file into a variable so that you can access it later. Although you could use the file_get_contents() function to perform this task, let's do it by hand; this is a good introduction to file access, because it shows all of the basic steps. Here's how you would place the contents of file.txt into the $file_data variable:

```php
<?php

$file_data = '';

$fd = fopen('file.txt', 'r');
if (!$fd) {
    echo "Error! Couldn't open the file.";
    die;
}

while (! feof($fd)) {
    $file_data .= fgets($fd, 5000);
```

```
    }

    fclose($fd);

?>
```

The fopen() function is an essential first step in most file access. It acts as a gateway between the system and PHP. When opening a file, you specify how you want to access the file. In this case, we open it for read access. You can also open a file for write access.

fopen() returns a *resource ID* that you use with other functions to perform file operations. In this case, we use fgets() and feof() to do the actual work.

fopen() has two parameters: the file's path and the mode. Here are the commonly useful modes (keep in mind that any of these can fail if you don't have the proper permissions for it).

r Open for reading only; start from the beginning of the file.

w Open for writing only (see the following section); start from the beginning of the file, and erase the contents of the file. If the file does not exist, attempt to create it.

x Create and open for writing only; start from the beginning of the file. If the file already exists, the fopen() call returns false. This option is supported in PHP 4.3.2 and later.

a- Open for writing only; start at the end of the file. If the file does not exist, attempt to create it.

The following file operations open the file for both reading and writing. Don't use them unless you really know what you're doing:

w+ Open for reading and writing; start from the beginning of the file, and erase the contents of the file if it has any. If the file does not exist, attempt to create it.

r+ Open for reading and writing; start from the beginning of the file.

a+ Open for reading and writing; start at the end of the file. If the file does not exist, attempt to create it.

x+ Create and open for reading and writing; start from the beginning of the file. If the file already exists, the fopen() function call returns false. This option is supported in PHP 4.3.2 and later.

Getting back to the script, $fd = fopen('file.txt', 'r') means *Open this file to read only and assign the resource ID to $fd*. To see if the open worked correctly, we just see if $fd has a value.

Now we're ready to do the real work in a loop. The feof() function tells us when we've hit the end of the file, so we use that as a test condition to break the loop. The fgets() function call here retrieves the next line of the file, up to 5,000 bytes' worth at a time. We append that to $file_data. When finished, we use fclose($fd) to free system resources and tell the system that we're finished with file access.

Hacking the Script

Many scripts process file data line by line instead of saving it into one huge variable. This comes up fairly often, especially when you're looking at lists of items generated by other programs. ("#55: Reading a Comma-Separated File" on page 101 shows you an example of when you'd want to examine each line individually.) To do this, just change the inside of the loop, as in this example, which prints every line that matches *bob*.

```
while (! feof($fd)) {
    $file_data = fgets($fd, 5000);
    if (strstr($file_data, 'bob') !== FALSE) {
        print $file_data;
    }
}
```

Notice how the `.=` append operator from the original script changed to the `=` assignment operator here. It's subtle but very important.

Depending on how your server is configured, you may be able to use `fopen()` to read data from a URL, such as this:

```
$fr = fopen('http://www.yahoo.com', 'r');
```

However, if you're running your own server, you should be very careful about allowing `fopen()` to access files outside your website; some PHP-specific worms have used `fopen()` in very nasty ways. Essentially, you have to be very careful about filenames—make sure that the user doesn't have any say in the filenames that `fopen()` accesses! You can shut down `fopen()` by setting `allow_url_fopen` to `false`, as shown in "Configuration Settings and the php.ini File" on page 20. For a more powerful alternative, use cURL to access websites, as shown in Chapter 11.

What Can Go Wrong?

The most common error occurs when PHP does not have permission to read the file. There are some files that PHP just shouldn't look at (password files, for example), and you may get an error message if you try to open one of these. Check the permissions, as shown in "File Permissions" on page 91.

This leads to discussion of a bigger issue: *never, ever allow a user to open a file before verifying that the user has any business opening that file.* Remember that you can't trust what the user is going to send to you. If you base filenames too closely on user data, it's entirely possible that a user could access any file on your site. Essentially, you need rules that absolutely restrict directory access for files on your site.

You should also verify data from files that users attempt to upload. See "#54: Uploading Images to a Directory" on page 97 for an example of how to verify file type, location, size, and more.

#51: Creating and Writing to a File

Here's how to write a string to a file:

```
<?
$file_data = "Hello, file.\nSecond line.";
$fd = fopen('file.txt', 'w');
if (!$fd) {
    echo "Error! Couldn't open/create the file.";
    die;
}
fwrite($fd, $file_data);
fclose($fd);
?>
```

Notice that this script explicitly includes newlines. When viewed on a Unix machine, the file looks like this:

```
Hello, file.
Second line.
```

The separator between the two lines is called a newline. On Unix and Macs, it's a single character represented in PHP as \n inside double quotes. However, in Windows and Macs, the newline is the \r\n sequence ("carriage return, then newline").

Therefore, if you actually care about cross-platform text file readability, you need to be a little careful. A Unix text file appears as one big line in Windows, and a Windows text file has a carriage return before the end of each line.

You can explicitly state the newline as \r\n if you like, but if you're really worried about portability, add a t to the end of the mode in fopen(), so the mode is wt. This automatically translates \n to \r\n on Windows.

#52: Checking to See If a File Exists

fopen() generates error messages if you're trying to open a file that doesn't exist, as do other functions such as unlink(), when you attempt to delete a nonexistent file. To see if a file exists before you perform a file operation, use the file_exists() function in a test condition:

```
<?
if (file_exists('file.txt')) {
    print 'OK, file.txt exists.';
}
```

As you can see, this function returns true if the file exists and false if it does not.

#53: Deleting Files

To remove a file on Unix, use the unlink() function:

```
<?
if (unlink("file.txt")) {
    echo "file.txt deleted.";
} else {
    echo "file.txt: delete failed.";
}
?>
```

You need the proper permissions to delete a file, of course. However, the biggest danger here is that you can delete a file that you didn't mean to delete. When you delete a file in Unix, it's gone; there's no undelete or trash can. The only way you might get something back is from your system administrator's backups.

And be careful here if you plan to have user actions deleting files. This is dangerous for every reason discussed and for every other file operation discussed so far.

#54: Uploading Images to a Directory

Periodically uploading 5 or 10 photos a week to a webserver is a bother. When I was updating my webserver, I had to save photos on my hard drive, start the FTP client, put them on the site, and then send the URL to anyone interested. There are a lot of image gallery programs that do this, but most are very complicated; I wanted to see if I could do something a little simpler.

Like all good lazy programmers, I decided to automate the process, coming up with a fairly foolproof system that allows users to upload pictures (and pictures only) into a directory. The features I wanted to incorporate would block excessively large images and generate HTML complete with height and width attributes. The first part of the system is a script called upload.html that takes the image input data:

```
<table border="0" cellpadding="10">
<form action="image_process.php" enctype="multipart/form-data" method="post">
<tr>
    <td valign=top><strong>Image file:</strong></td>
    <td><input name="upfile" type="file"><br>
        Image files must be in JPEG, GIF, or PNG format.
    </td>
</tr>
<tr>
    <td valign="top"><strong>Target directory:</strong></td>
    <td>
     <select name="location">
       <option value="article" selected>Article Images</option>
```

```
        <option value="banners">Banners/Advertisements</option>
      </select>
    </td>
</tr>
<tr>
    <td valign="top"><strong>Filename (Optional):</strong></td>
    <td><input name="newname" type="text" size="64" maxlength="64"></td>
</tr>
<tr>
    <td colspan="2">
        <div align="center"><input type="submit" value="Upload Image"></div>
    </td>
</tr>
</form>
</table>
```

Here's the image_process.php script that processes this form. The first thing we need to do is set some configuration variables:

```php
<?php
/* Configuration */

$root = "/home/www/wcphp/images";              /* Image directory root */
$urlroot = "http://www.example.com/images";    /* URL root */
$max_width = 420;                              /* Max width */
$max_height = 600;                             /* Max height */
$overwrite_images = false;                      /* Allow overwrite */

/* Permitted subdirectories */
$target_dirs = array("article", "banners");

/* End config */
```

Set the $root variable to where you want to store images and the $urlroot to where you'd go to look at them from a web browser. The items in $target_dirs are subdirectories in $root. These are the only locations where you will allow users to store images.

With the configuration out of the way, let's first check to see if the script will work—it all depends on the availability of the getimagesize() function:

```php
if (!function_exists(getimagesize)) {
    die("getimagesize() required.");
}
```

Extracting the field information from the form follows standard procedure:

```php
/* Get upload information. */
$location = strval($_POST['location']);
$newname = strval($_POST['newname']);
$upfile = $_FILES['upfile']['tmp_name'];
$upfile_name = $_FILES['upfile']['name'];
```

We need to determine what we want to call the file on the server. When doing so, we want to ensure that there are no weird characters in the name and that we won't be able to leave the target directory by adding a bunch of slashes (/). You can do this in one shot with a regular expression that removes any character you don't recognize. After you're finished, $newname contains the new name for the uploaded file:

```
/* Delete any unwanted characters in the target name. */
if ($newname) {
    $newname = preg_replace('/[^A-Za-z0-9_.-]/', '', $newname);
} else {
    $newname = preg_replace('/[^A-Za-z0-9_.-]/', '', $upfile_name);
}
```

It's time to start validating the parameters. First, we check to see if the target subdirectory is in our valid list:

```
/* Validate parameters. */
if (!in_array($location, $target_dirs)) {
    /* Invalid location */
    die("invalid target directory.");
} else {
    $urlroot .= "/$location";
}
```

Here's a sanity check to make sure that PHP actually uploaded a file:

```
if (!$upfile) {
    /* No file */
    die("no file for upload.");
}
```

Now it's time to validate the data itself. We initialize the file types that we want to accept and then use getimagesize() to get the dimensions of the uploaded image and its type ($attr appears later in the script).

```
/* Verify file type. */
$file_types = array(
    "image/jpeg"        => "jpg",
    "image/pjpeg"       => "jpg",
    "image/gif"         => "gif",
    "image/png"         => "png",
);
$width = null;
$height = null;

/* Extract MIME type and size for the image. */
$img_info = getimagesize($upfile);
$upfile_type = $img_info["mime"];
list($width, $height, $t, $attr) = $img_info;
```

Using the parameters just extracted, we make sure that the image is in an acceptable format, figure out what its suffix should be, and ensure that it is not too large:

```
/* Validate type. */
if (!$file_types[$upfile_type]) {
    die("image must be in JPEG, GIF, or PNG format.");
} else {
    $file_suffix = $file_types[$upfile_type];
}

/* Validate size. */
if ($width > $max_width || $height > $max_height) {
    die("size $width x $height exceeds maximum $max_width x $max_height.");
}
```

Every now and then, someone uploads a file with an incorrect suffix. This isn't really that big of a deal, but it does mess up the MIME type when the server sends it. Because we now know the correct suffix, we coerce that suffix by chopping off any possible incorrect suffix and adding our own. Someone may also mistype a suffix, and this step also corrects that by simply tacking on the correct suffix. For example, foo.jopg might become foo.jopg.jpg. Although you also could try to correct for that, you would find yourself second-guessing users who really ought to learn how to type.

After determining this final name for the uploaded file, we assign its full pathname to $new_fullpath:

```
/* Force file suffix. */
$newname = preg_replace('/\.(jpe?g|gif|png)$/i', "");
$newname .= $file_suffix;
$new_fullpath = "$root/$location/$newname";
```

Now that we have the final name, we can verify that the file does not already exist when set to no-overwrite mode:

```
if ((!$overwrite_images) && file_exists($new_fullpath)) {
    die("file exists; will not overwrite.");
}
```

Now it's time to copy the file into its final location and make sure the copy was successful:

```
/* Copy the file into final location. */
if (!copy($upfile, $new_fullpath)) {
    die("copy failed.");
}
```

If we've made it this far, then the upload was successful, and all we need to do is print some HTML to give the user a link:

```
$image_url = "$urlroot/$newname";

/* Display status. */
print "HTML for image:</strong><br><textarea cols=\"80\" rows=\"4\">";
print "<img src=\"$image_url\" $attr alt=\"$upfile_name\" border=\"0\"/>";
print "</textarea><br>";
print '<a href="upload.html">Upload another image?</a>';?>
```

Using the Script

This script requires that all target directories in $target_dirs be writeable by PHP. In addition, you need the GD module, a PHP add-in that allows PHP to analyze and create image files. Most servers have this installed by default, but if yours does not, refer back to "#18: Adding Extensions to PHP" on page 27.

That's it; all you need to do is point the browser at upload.html, and PHP will do the rest.

What Can Go Wrong?

Aside from the usual permissions problems, the biggest issue is security. As it stands, any schmo who has access to this script's URL can upload as many images as they like and possibly overwrite yours. If this script is outside a firewall, you may want to combine this script with a login function to prevent unauthorized access, as shown in "#63: A Simple Login System" on page 116.

Hacking the Script

You can impose a cap on the size of any given file by looking at the $_FILES['upfile']['size'] variable. Just put in a line like this:

```
If ($_FILES['upfile']['size'] > $max_size) {
    $fatal_error = "This file is larger than $max_size bytes.";
}
```

NOTE   *You may also want to have a look at "#13: Preventing Users from Uploading Large Files" on page 25, which shows you how to set a global upload file size limit.*

#55: Reading a Comma-Separated File

One common programming task is to transform data from Excel spreadsheets into some useful form, such as HTML or rows in a MySQL table. If we all had to work in Excel (XLS) format, then this would be a real problem. Fortunately, in both Excel and OpenOffice.org, you can export an Excel file into CSV (comma-separated value) format. CSV format is a fancy way to say that it's a text file with one line per data row, with commas between the fields in the row. It looks like this:

```
"Airport","City","Activity"
"LON","London","Museums"
"PAR","Paris","Dining"
"SLC","Salt Lake City","Skiing"
```

Although you may think that this is just a matter of grabbing lines and splitting them using a comma as a delimiter, you have to worry about quotes, backslashes, and other minor details of the format. However, most languages have a built-in to deal with this stuff, and PHP is no exception. Processing CSV files is a breeze with the built-in fgetcsv() function. It works just like fgets(), except that it returns an array containing the current line's row values instead of a string. Here's a very simple script to process an uploaded CSV file from the csvfile field in a form:

```php
<table>
<tr>
  <th>Field 1</th>
  <th>Field 2</th>
  <th>Field 3</th>
</tr>
<?php

$fn = $_FILES["csvfile"]["tmp_name"];

$fd = fopen($fn, "r");

while (!feof($fd)) {
    $fields = fgetcsv($fd);
    print "<tr>";
    print "<td>$fields[0]</td><td>$fields[1]</td><td>$fields[2]</td>";
    print "</tr>";
}
fclose($fd);
?>
</table>
```

As you can see, this script prints the first three columns of the CSV file in HTML table format.

Sometimes you'll get a tab-delimited file instead of a CSV file. To read one of those, just change the line with fgetcsv() to something like this:

```php
$fields = fgetcsv($fd, 0, "\t");
```

The third parameter is the delimiter; be sure to use double quotes with \t. That second parameter is the maximum length of line in the CSV file. Set it to 0 if you don't want a length limit.

8

USER AND SESSION TRACKING

The World Wide Web's initial design was little more than a series of static pages and media. The design made it easy to publish and navigate pages, but the Web truly became useful when sites began to offer dynamic content. Much of this content is specific to a session—a shopping cart, for instance, is session data; it is generally unique to one browser (or user).

The tools and techniques for tracking web sessions are afterthoughts and hacks—ones that happen to do a somewhat reasonable job. Sometimes things get messed up, and you must be careful about security (as ever), but PHP can remove some of the complexity for you.

Using Cookies and Sessions to Track User Data

To find out what a specific user is doing on your site, you need to store information about that user, such as the username, password, time between visits, preferences, and so on. In web programming, two popular techniques for this are cookies and sessions.

Cookies

Cookies are small pieces of data that you store on the user's computer. When the user accesses more than one page on your site, the user's browser sends any valid cookies on those accesses back to your server. Because storing any kind of data on a user's computer without her knowledge is a potential security risk, you don't have direct control over how to store cookies. There are certain rules that the browser (and user) sets up, and if you follow the rules, the browser will accept your cookies and will send them back under the correct circumstances. An accepted cookie is said to be *set*.

Advantages

- Cookies can store information for years.
- Cookies work well with the kind of distributed, load-balanced webservers necessary for high-traffic sites, because all of the data is on the user's computer.

Disadvantages

- You need to be careful to follow the rules or lots of browsers will not accept your cookies, and they won't tell you of that refusal.
- Cookies are limited in size (it's generally best not to exceed 512Kb).
- Users can easily delete the cookies if they want to.
- Cookies are generally specific to one user on one computer. If a user switches to another computer, he generally will not use any of the old cookies.

Sessions

Sessions consist of a unique session ID and some sort of storage mechanism on your server. Because the data is on your server, the user doesn't get a chance to manipulate it.

Advantages

- Even though most sessions work by setting the session ID in a cookie, PHP and other web programming systems have ways to make sessions work without cookies. Therefore, this method almost always works.
- You can store as much session data as you like.
- Users cannot typically view or edit session data, and if they do, you have control over that editing process.

Disadvantages

- Sessions are normally specific to one browser window or one browser process. When you close that window, unless you store the session ID as a persistent cookie, the user won't get the old data back. However, with a login system, you can associate a session ID with a username.

- Out of the box on PHP, sessions are server specific. If you have a sales server and a content server, the sales server won't see any session data from the content server. You can customize the session storage system to solve this problem.

- Because the session ID is data that a user reads and sends, unless you take precautions, it's possible for snoopers to get access to sessions.

In abstract terms, you can think of sessions as enhanced cookies. There's still certain data (such as the session ID) that the user's computer gets in some way, but the real data is always on your server. There are many different implementations of session technology, but the basic idea is always the same.

Remember, though, if there's some data that you don't want users to read or modify, you should put it in a session, not a cookie. You need to do the same verification process for cookies that you would for any form data, because it comes from the client and therefore is easy to fabricate.

#56: Creating a "Welcome Back, *Username*!" Message with Cookies

One cheap parlor trick that many websites employ is displaying "Welcome back" to returning users. If you tell the site your name, it can greet you by name.

To illustrate one way to do this, here is a script that can store user information in a cookie and display the cookie if available:

```php
<?php
if (isset($_REQUEST["user_name"])) {
    setcookie("stored_user_name", $_REQUEST["user_name"], time() + 604800, "/");
    $_COOKIE["stored_user_name"] = $_REQUEST["user_name"];
}
if (isset($_COOKIE["stored_user_name"])) {
    $user = $_COOKIE["stored_user_name"];
    print "Welcome back, <b>$user</b>!";
} else {
    ?>
    <form method="post">
    User name: <input type="text" name="user_name" />
    </form>
    <?php
}?>
```

Accessing and storing cookies in PHP involve two separate mechanisms. You can read cookies that the client sends to you through the $_COOKIE array. This works like the $_POST and $_GET arrays.

To set cookies, use the setcookie() function, which has three required parameters:

- **The cookie name.** This script uses stored_user_name.

- **The cookie value.**

- **When the cookie should expire on the user's computer, as a Unix time-stamp.** This script uses time()+604800—seven days from the current time (see Chapter 6 for more detail on timestamps).

There are also three optional parameters:

A path to limit the places on your site where this cookie is valid.
This works like a directory; for example, if you want the cookie to be valid only for everything under /content/ on your site, use /content/ as this parameter. If you want the cookie to be valid everywhere on your site, use /.

A domain where the cookie is valid.
Let's say that you have www.example.com and sales.example.com hosts, and you want the cookie to be valid for both. To achieve this, use .example.com as the domain parameter. Don't bother with this if you have only one webserver host in your domain.

A setting for secure connections.
Using 1 as this parameter specifies that the browser should send the cookie only if the connection is secure.

What Can Go Wrong?

There are a number of problems that frequently occur when setting and retrieving cookies:

You sent data to the user's browser before calling setcookie().
Cookie request information is in the HTTP header of a response from a webserver. Therefore, you can't send any real document data to the client before you call setcookie(), that is, no printing or other operations that cause output. With warnings turned on, PHP tells you when you've made this mistake.

A common cause of this problem is being sloppy about whitespace in your PHP files. If you have any blank lines or spaces before the <? that starts the PHP code section, this problem will happen. This situation also applies to any files that you include before calling setcookie(); further-more, included files can't have any whitespace after the closing ?> marker.

The user's browser rejects the cookie.
If the browser doesn't accept the cookie, you won't get any feedback. To check for a cookie, use isset() to see if there is anything in the $_COOKIE[] array slot. The most common cause of a browser rejecting a cookie is an

incorrect domain (browsers typically do not accept cookies for domains that don't match the requesting server host).

Someone throws in a bad parameter.

Cookies, like anything else that the client sends you, are easily fabricated. Don't trust their values; verify them just as you would any form data.

You're trying to store an array in a cookie variable.

You can't do that. You can, however, use a serialized array (see "#5: Turning an Array into a Nonarray Variable That Can Be Restored Later" on page 12).

#57: Using Sessions to Temporarily Store Data

A fairly common user interface design has a user entering a fairly extensive amount of data over several forms. You also may want to store a set of data for as long as the user's browser is open (for example, for a shopping cart). Though this is technically possible with hidden form fields, it's not desirable in most cases because of its complexity and browser-state problems.

PHP has a built-in *session management* system that you can use to store and access data on a per-browser basis. It does most of the dirty work of setting cookies (or setting a session ID parameter) and storing the data somewhere on your server. All you need to do in your PHP scripts is start the session manager with the session_start() function and then access session data with the $_SESSION array.

Here's a form that uses session management to capture, summarize, and edit data. Let's start with a simple form script. The first part starts the session and extracts existing session data:

```
<?
session_start();

$name = $_SESSION["name"];
$color = $_SESSION["color"];
```

New users won't have these variables set, but if they return to this form at any point, this part of the script captures their old values. When printing the form, we use those old values as defaults:

```
print '<form action="sessionview.php" method="post">';
print 'What is your name? ';
print '<input name="name" type="text" value="' . $name . '" /><br/>';
print 'What is your favorite color? ';
print '<input name="color" type="text" value="' . $color . '" /><br/>';
print '<input type="submit"/ >';
print '<input type="submit" name="clear" value="Clear Details" />';

?>
```

Notice that there is an extra submit button for clearing session values (you'll see how this works soon). Here's the sessionview.php script that stores the form data and gives the user the opportunity to go back and edit the values. First, we start the session and check to see if the name and/or color have been sent as form data. If they have, we set those values as session variables:

```
<?
session_start();

if ($_REQUEST["name"]) {
    $_SESSION["name"] = $_REQUEST["name"];
}
if ($_REQUEST["color"]) {
    $_SESSION["color"] = $_REQUEST["color"];
}
```

The next part checks to see if the user pressed the Clear Details button on the form. If this is the case, then we use unset() to clear the session values:

```
if ($_REQUEST["clear"]) {
    unset($_SESSION["name"]);
    unset($_SESSION["color"]);
}
```

Now we know that the $_SESSION array contains all of the correct values, so we can print the user's information based on those values:

```
$name = $_SESSION["name"];
$color = $_SESSION["color"];

if ($name) {
    print "Your name is <b>$name</b>.<br />";
}
if ($color) {
    print "Your favorite color is <b>$color</b>.<br />";
}
```

Finally, we give the user a chance to go back and edit the details or clear the values. We've done all of the work in our scripts already, so we just need to provide hyperlinks to the correct places:

```
print '<a href="sessionform.php">Edit details</a>';
print ' | <a href="sessionview.php?clear=1">Clear values</a>';
?>
```

This is a very simple example, but as you can see, it illustrates how sessions can make your life a lot easier when you need to create a multipart form or track other state information.

What Can Go Wrong?

Just as you would do when setting a cookie, you must place session_start() early in the script before you send any data, so that the server can set up the session ID on the client. Otherwise, the client won't accept the session ID, and the server will be unable to associate the client with a session.

#58: Checking to See If a User's Browser Accepts Cookies

To see if a browser accepts cookies, you must check in two distinct steps, in two distinct web requests. The client's browser must make two requests because the browser sets a cookie only when it gets a response from the first request.

You can serve both requests with one script, but you have to be careful not to put the browser in an infinite loop. The idea is to check for the cookie, and if the cookie is not set, you must try to set it and reload the page. But you want to reload only once, so you also have to tell the script that it is doing a reload to prevent it from loading yet again if the cookie is not set.

This is a small script, but because you run the risk of infinitely reloading pages, you have to be careful. The first thing we do is check to see if the cookie we're testing is already set. If so, since the browser supports cookies, there's nothing left to do:

```php
<?php
if (isset($_COOKIE["test"])) {
    print "Cookies enabled.";
```

If this cookie does not exist, then there are two possible situations: First, the browser may not accept cookies. However, we won't know for sure until the *second* time we load the page, and we need to know when the browser has reloaded the page. To achieve this, we'll set a GET parameter called testing on the second access. If this parameter exists and the cookie doesn't exist, then we know that the browser isn't sending cookies:

```php
} else {
    if (isset($_REQUEST["testing"])) {
        print "Cookies disabled.";
```

However, if the cookie doesn't exist and the testing parameter does not exist, then this is the first time that the browser has accessed the page. Therefore, we want to set the cookie and then reload the page, this time setting the testing parameter to indicate that it's a second access. You'll see how the Location header works in the following section.

```
    } else {
        setcookie("test", "1", 0, "/");
        header("Location: $_SERVER[PHP_SELF]?testing=1");
    }
}
?>
```

It's extremely important that you do not forget to include the testing parameter. If you omit it, the page will reload infinitely if the browser does not support cookies.

This script isn't terribly intuitive to read, because the first pieces that the user encounters do not correspond to the first lines of code. However, it is so small that you can easily understand it entirely, and once you do that, you should have no problems with it.

#59: Redirecting Users to Different Pages

Redirecting users to new pages is a fact of life when programming dynamic websites. The primary reason is that you often need to redirect a user after making session state changes. For example, when you add an item to a shopping cart, you want the user to go to a page such as the current shopping cart, and you don't want to add another one of the same item to the cart again if you reload that shopping cart page. Most sites achieve this with a script that processes the state change and then redirects to the page that they want the user to see.

There are essentially two ways to do it. The first and preferred way is to use the HTTP Location header, like this:

```
<?
    header("Location: new_page.php");
?>
```

The header() function sends raw HTTP headers to the user's browser. Therefore, you need to do this before sending any other output to the browser, just as you would when setting a cookie.

There are two advantages to this method. First, it is instant, and the intermediate script does not appear in a web browser's history. Second, because it is HTTP based, it does not require a web browser to process; automatic web crawlers and programs such as wget understand it.

However, if you would like to show an intermediate page to the user with a delay, you need to use a different method that uses the HTML <meta> tag. It's pretty simple; to send a user to a different page after displaying the current page for five seconds, put the following in your HTML header:

```
<meta http-equiv="Refresh" content="5;URL= new_page.php" />
```

All web browsers understand this, but automatic page crawlers sometimes do not. In addition, this intermediate page will show up in the user's browser history.

#60: Forcing a User to Use SSL-Encrypted Pages

When handling credit card information, you want to guarantee that all card information always goes through an SSL (Secure Socket Layer) connection.

If a user types www.example.com in his web browser, he gets http://www .example.com/, not https://www.example.com/. This isn't a problem if all of your forms specifically refer to pages under https://www.example.com/, but it's difficult to ensure that and to maintain it if your hostname happens to change.

Here is a simple function to see if a user is connecting via SSL or not:

```
function is_SSL() {
    /* Checks to see whether the page is in secure mode */
    if ($_SERVER['SERVER_PORT'] == "443") {
        return true;
    } else {
        return false;
    }
}
```

This function works by checking the port through which the client connected to the server (SSL is port 443). If the access is not secure and it should be, you can use $_SERVER['PHP_SELF'] and the header() function described in the preceding section to redirect to a secure version of the page.

#61: Extracting Client Information

Webservers can extract information about their connecting clients by looking at TCP/IP status and HTTP headers. You can access the client's IP address and browser version fairly easily through PHP variables. However, like almost anything the client sends you, this information is completely useless for session tracking. IP addresses aren't unique because of proxies and Network Address Translation (NAT), and browser versions can be completely bogus.

This information is, however, good for finding basic statistics about your users. A few bogus headers here and there aren't going to matter if you're looking at 100,000 accesses.

The following function extracts an IP address. The first part is relatively simple, because it looks into what the server thinks it knows about the client:

```
function get_ip() {
    /* First, look for an IP address from the server. */
    if (!empty($_SERVER["REMOTE_ADDR"])) {
        $client_ip = $_SERVER["REMOTE_ADDR"];
    }
```

Depending on how much you actually care, this may be all you need. However, if you feel some pressing need to see if a user is coming from a proxy server, the following code looks for a proxy server and checks for an underlying client IP address:

```
/* Look for proxy servers. */
if ($_SERVER["HTTP_CLIENT_IP"]) {
    $proxy_ip = $_SERVER["HTTP_CLIENT_IP"];
} else if ($_SERVER["HTTP_X_FORWARDED_FOR"]) {
    $proxy_ip = $_SERVER["HTTP_X_FORWARDED_FOR"];
}
```

The problem with looking for clients behind proxy servers is that many users employ a proxy because they're behind a private network. An IP address on a private network is useless to you because it's not unique and provides no demographic value. In this case, it's better to use the original IP address. The following code looks for a valid IP address, and if the address is valid, it determines whether it's on a private network. If the network is private, we use the original IP address:

```
/* Look for a real IP address underneath proxies. */
if ($proxy_ip) {
    if (preg_match("/^([0-9]+\.[0-9]+\.[0-9]+\.[0-9]+)/",
        $proxy_ip, $ip_list)) {
        $private_ip = array(
            '/^0\./',
            '/^127\.0\.0\.1/',
            '/^192\.168\..*/',
            '/^172\.16\..*/',
            '/^10\.\.*/',
            '/^224\.\.*/',
            '/^240\.\.*/',
        );
        $client_ip = preg_replace($private_ip, $client_ip, $ip_list[1]);
    }
}
```

Finally, we return what we think the IP address is:

```
    return $client_ip;
}
```

PHP stores the user agent information in the $_SERVER['HTTP_USER_AGENT'] variable. Unfortunately, this string is convoluted and does not follow a standard. For example, here is what you'd get with Internet Explorer on Windows:

```
Mozilla/4.0 (compatible; MSIE 6.0; Windows NT 5.1; SV1)
```

In Opera, it looks like this:

```
Mozilla/4.0 (compatible; MSIE 6.0; Windows NT 5.1) Opera 7.54 [en]
```

And here's Firefox on Linux:

```
Mozilla/5.0 (X11; U; Linux i686; en-US; rv:1.8.1.4) Gecko/20070515 Firefox/
2.0.0.4
```

The reason why user agent strings look like blatant lies is that most browsers try to trick the server into believing that they're something else. Here, the Internet Explorer user agent claims to be Mozilla (the code name for Netscape Navigator). Opera calls itself Mozilla, and then it says that it's Explorer (MSIE 6.0), and at the end, it finally tells you that it's Opera. Although this behavior is completely idiotic, it's not half as stupid as optimizing pages for particular browsers in the first place.

The only pieces of the user agent string that you should actually care about are the browser, version, and operating system, because these tell you something about your users. For example, if you see an unusually large proportion of Mac users, part of your market base probably likes to buy expensive gadgets for the sole purpose of looking stylish. Here's a function that tries to extract the browser and operating system information into a usable form. It's ugly, but in this case, we have to fight ugly with ugly.

First, let's initialize the output array and put the browser identification string into the $agent variable:

```
function find_browser() {
// Determine OS, version, and type of client browsers.
    $browser_info = array(
        "name"    => "Unknown",
        "version" => "Unknown",
        "OS"      => "Unknown",
    );
    // Get the User Agent.
    if (!empty($_SERVER["HTTP_USER_AGENT"])) {
        $agent = $_SERVER["HTTP_USER_AGENT"];
    }
```

Now, let's look for the user's operating system. This is relatively easy, because the operating system strings are unique:

```
    // Find operating system.
    if (preg_match('/win/i', $agent)) {
        $browser_info["OS"] = "Windows";
    } else if (preg_match('/mac/i', $agent)) {
        $browser_info["OS"] = "Macintosh";
    } else if (preg_match('/linux/i', $agent)) {
        $browser_info["OS"] = "Linux";
    }
```

Then the tough part of figuring out the browser details begins. The order in which we check for browsers is important, because some browser strings say that they are several other browsers. The biggest offender is

Opera, so we start with that one. The worst part about Opera is that it can state its version in one of two ways—with a slash or without. We try both:

```php
if (preg_match('/opera/i', $agent)) {
    // Must start with Opera, since it matches IE string
        $browser_info["name"] = "Opera";
        $agent = stristr($agent, "Opera");
        if (strpos("/", $agent)) {
            $agent = explode("/", $agent);
            $browser_info["version"] = $agent[1];
        } else {
            $agent = explode(" ", $agent);
            $browser_info["version"] = $agent[1];
        }
```

Next on the list of suspects is Internet Explorer, because it claims to be Mozilla. Pulling out its version is easier, because the only thing you may need to remove from the version string is a semicolon at the end:

```php
} else if (preg_match('/msie/i', $agent)) {
        $browser_info["name"] = "Internet Explorer";
        $agent = stristr($agent, "msie");
        $agent = explode(" ", $agent);
        $browser_info["version"] = str_replace(";", "", $agent[1]);
```

As of yet, no other browser claims to be Firefox, but Firefox is a version of Mozilla, so now is a good time to check for this browser. Notice how extracting the version is much easier here:

```php
} else if (preg_match('/firefox/i', $agent)) {
        $browser_info["name"] = "Firefox";
        $agent = stristr($agent, "Firefox");
        $agent = explode("/", $agent);
        $browser_info["version"] = $agent[1];
```

Safari claims to use something "like Gecko," the Mozilla engine. However, because we use Gecko as a test for the various versions of Mozilla, we need to check for Safari first:

```php
} else if (preg_match('/safari/i', $agent)) {
        $browser_info["name"] = "Safari";
        $agent = stristr($agent, "Safari");
        $agent = explode("/", $agent);
        $browser_info["version"] = $agent[1];
```

Netscape Navigator, of course, is a version of Mozilla:

```php
} else if (preg_match('/netscape/i', $agent)) {
        $browser_info["name"] = "Netscape Navigator";
        $agent = stristr($agent, "Netscape");
```

```
    $agent = explode("/", $agent);
    $browser_info["version"] = $agent[1];
```

Finally, if we're looking at a Gecko-based browser, we know that it's probably Mozilla or a variant:

```
} else if (preg_match('/Gecko/i', $agent)){
    $browser_info["name"]= 'Mozilla';
    $agent = stristr($agent, "rv");
    $agent = explode(":", $agent);
    $agent = explode(")", $agent[1]);
    $browser_info["version"] = $agent[1];
}
return $browser_info;
}
```

As previously mentioned, this function is about as clumsy as they come, because it just haphazardly pokes away at the user agent string until it finds information that looks halfway intelligible. Even when you have this function, you still need to store the information somewhere and make sense of it. If you have access to your own web log files, you should consider a log file analyzer solution such as awstats (http://awstats.sourceforge.net/) that can extract a wealth of information, including IP addresses and browsers.

#62: Session Timeouts

Users should not stay logged in to high-security sites for prolonged periods of time. If someone walks away from a session on a site such as PayPal, someone else could walk up to the computer and move around some cash. Therefore, such sites use session timeouts to automatically log out users who haven't done anything for a short period of time (such as 10 minutes). It's important to note that you shouldn't do this if the site does not require such high security, because it is annoying to users.

Here are two functions that implement session timeouts. Notice that the timeout variables are in session variables—you can't trust this information to a browser, so you must keep it on your own server. The first function validates the login session:

```
function login_validate() {
    /* Set the timeout on a login session. */
    /* Default timeout is ten minutes (600 seconds). */
    @session_start();
    $timeout = 600;
    $_SESSION["expires_by"] = time() + $timeout;
}
```

NOTE   *If you're confident that the session has already started by the time you call this function, you can remove the @session_start() call.*

The second function checks the current login to see if the session has expired. If the session is valid, it resets the session timeout:

```
function login_check() {
    @session_start();
    /* Checks for session activity timeout. */
    $exp_time = intval($_SESSION["expires_by"]);
    if (time() < $exp_time) {
        /* Session still valid; refresh the time. */
        login_validate();
        return true;
    } else {
        /* Session expired; remove session variable. */
        unset($_SESSION["expires_by"]);
        return false;
    }
}
```

The reason for two separate functions is that when the user logs in for the first time, you need to set the timeout for the first time with login_validate(). Even though setting the timeout is a very simple process, it's important to be consistent, because you may make things more complicated later.

Using login_check() is fairly simple. Here's an example of how you would protect pages that you need to access with a login at login.php:

```
<?
if (!login_check()) {
    header("Location: login.php");
    exit(0);
}
?>
```

As with any session-based user tracking, remember that you must run session_start() at the beginning of the script, before any headers. These functions ignore errors from session_start() because there may be previous invocations of session_start().

#63: A Simple Login System

On certain websites, you want a simple authentication system for administrative purposes. Smaller sites with just a couple of administrators don't require a fully fledged login system with individual usernames; you just want to keep out the riffraff. One example of such a site would be "#54: Uploading Images to a Directory" on page 97.

Here is the code for single-user authentication. The general idea is to set a session variable named $_SESSION["auth"] to completed when logged in.

We define the password first. As usual, we do not store plaintext passwords. This one is an MD5 hash—you need to change the string to one that you generate for yourself. You'll see how to do this shortly.

```
<?    $enc_passwd = "206bfaa5da7422d2f497239dcf8b96f3";
```

Now let's start by defining what to do when someone logs out (signified by a logout parameter). First, we set the session variable to incomplete, send the user to a generic page (here, index.php), and exit:

```
session_start();
if ($_REQUEST["logout"]) {
    $_SESSION["auth"] = "incomplete";
    header("Location: index.php");
    exit(0);
}
```

If the user is logging in, she'll do it through a pwd parameter. To see if the password is correct, we MD5-hash the parameter and compare the hash against the encrypted password. If everything checks out, we validate the session variable and send the user to a home page. You may not need to do this redirection depending on how your site sends form parameters. However, the danger is always that you may be trying to change something that requires a login, and then you log in, but as you are logging in, you lose the original parameters that you were trying to work with. It's safer to send new logins to some sort of home page.

```
if ($_REQUEST["pwd"]) {
    if (md5($_REQUEST["pwd"]) == $enc_passwd) {
        $_SESSION["auth"] = "completed";
        header("Location: index.php");
        exit(0);
    }
}
```

If we've gotten to this point, we know that we're not logging in or out, so all we have to do is check to see if the user is already logged in. Remember that this is in the $_SESSION["auth"] variable, so we check that. If the user is not logged in, we give the user the opportunity to log in by printing a login form, and then exit. You could also do this by redirecting the user to a special login page if you want to make it look better, but it's important that you always exit after redirecting or printing the form. Past this point you don't want to let PHP do anything that a logged-in user is able to do!

```
$authed = $_SESSION["auth"];
if ($authed != "completed") {
    ?><html><head></head><body>
      <form method="post">
      Enter password: <input type="password" name="pwd"/>
      </form>
      </body></html><?php
    exit(0);
}
?>
```

To use this script, call it login.php and require it at the beginning of any script that should have authentication. When a client first encounters the page, the script prints a login form and exits before giving any other code a chance to run.

To set a new password for the script, run this script to generate the new password's hash, and then set the $enc_passwd string to the output:

```
<?
print md5("newpassword");

?>
```

Remember that this is a very simple login system. You can augment it by adding the session timeout code from the preceding section, but if you find yourself asking for more features, you probably want to start from a fully tested login system. There are several free systems available on the Internet—they're definitely worth checking out.

9

WORKING WITH EMAIL

You won't need to manipulate much email in PHP, but one thing that you will need to do is send confirmation messages to users and administrators about account settings, orders, and so on. The easiest way to send email in PHP is with the mail() function. If your mail server is set up correctly, and you need only to send messages to yourself, then this is probably the only function you'll ever need.

Here's a simple script to illustrate how mail() works. Replace user@example .com with a working email address:

```
if (mail('user@example.com', 'PHP email test', 'It worked!')) {
    echo "Mail sent.";
} else {
    echo "Mail delivery failed.";
}
```

If this script says *Mail sent.* when run, check the target email to verify that it actually did work. The subject should be *PHP email test* and the body should be *It worked!*

The mail() function, like any other system that sends email, is susceptible to problems in the mail-delivery system. You may need to fix your mail server's configuration to get things working. However, because there is so much junk in email now, a malformed or irregular mail header may cause a remote server to reject your email without telling you. In addition, when you send attachments or add HTML text, you have to do a lot more work. The next section shows you how overcome these problems with PHPMailer.

#64: Using PHPMailer to Send Mail

PHPMailer is an open source email package that supports attachments, multiple recipients, SMTP authentication, and a large number of other features. It's well tested and relatively easy to use and upgrade. You need only include the core PHPMailer file as a part of your script, and you're ready to go.

Installing PHPMailer

Just follow these steps to install PHPMailer:

1. Download the core PHPMailer files from http://phpmailer .sourceforge.net/.

2. Create a directory called *phpmailer* on your server to store the core PHPMailer files.

3. Extract the PHPMailer files into the phpmailer directory.

4. Determine your mail transport method. PHPMailer has three different methods to send email: mail, sendmail, and smtp. The default is mail, which uses the PHP mail() function discussed in the preceding section. It's the easiest to configure, assuming that your webserver's mail is configured correctly. If this method doesn't work, you have two remaining options:

    a. You can provide PHPMailer with an SMTP server to talk to. SMTP stands for Simple Mail Transfer Protocol, the most common protocol for transporting email messages. To configure PHPMailer for SMTP, you need the SMTP server hostname. If the server requires SMTP authentication (as most do), you need a username and password for that server. Your ISP will be able to tell you the details about its SMTP server settings.

    b. If your webserver uses sendmail or a package with a sendmail-compatible binary (such as Postfix) you can configure PHPMailer to use this to send mail. You need to know the sendmail binary location where the core sendmail executable resides. It's usually /usr/sbin/sendmail or /usr/lib/sendmail.

5. Adjust the PHPMailer default settings by editing the class.phpmailer.php file. You'll want to change the settings in the Public Variables section at the top of the file. The most important settings are as follows:

> `var $Mailer = "mail";` The method PHPMailer uses to send email. Set this to `mail`, `sendmail`, or `smtp`, as determined in step 4.

> `var $From = "root@localhost";` The default origin email address.

> `var $FromName = "Root User";` The default name associated with the default email address.

> `var $Host = "";` The SMTP server you want to use when using SMTP to connect. Check with your ISP for details. You can list multiple SMTP servers separated by semicolons (;) in case the first SMTP server is down or rejects the email.

> `var $SMTPAuth = false;` If your SMTP server requires authentication to send emails, set this to `true`. If you set this, you must also set the following two variables.

> `var $Username = "";` When using SMTP authentication, the username on the SMTP server.

> `var $Password = "";` The password associated with `$Username`, if necessary.

> `var $Helo = "";` The name of your webserver, such as www.example.com.

After changing any necessary configuration variables, you're ready to see a simple script that sends a test message.

Using the Script

Make sure the class.phpmailer.php file is in your include path, and try this script:

```php
<?php
include_once("class.phpmailer.php");
$mail = new PHPMailer;
$mail->ClearAddresses();
$mail->AddAddress('theferrett@theferrett.com', 'The Ferrett');
$mail->From = 'you@example.com';
$mail->FromName = 'Your Name';
$mail->Subject = 'Test Message Subject';
$mail->Body = 'This is the test message body.';
if ($mail->Send()) {
    echo "Message sent.";
} else {
    echo $mail->ErrorInfo;
}
?>
```

PHPMailer has an object-oriented interface. You need to create an object ($mail in the preceding example) and then set some attributes and call some methods to set up the message. When you've finished, use the object's Send() method to send the message. This method returns true if PHPMailer was able to hand the message to its delivery agent. If there was a problem at this stage, you'll find the details in the ErrorInfo variable.

Here is an overview of the methods and attributes used in the example:

`$mail->AddAddress(`*`email_address, real_name`*`)`

Add a recipient for the current message. *email_address* is the address of the recipient, and *real_name* is the real name of the recipient (or, at least, what you'd rather call the recipient).

`$mail->ClearAddresses()`

This line clears the current recipient address list. Because the AddAddress() method doesn't remove previous addresses, you run the risk of sending a message to someone many times if you send messages in a loop using a single PHPMailer object. Therefore, you should get into the habit of clearing the recipient list before you do anything with a message or after you call the Send() method.

`$mail->isHTML = `*`true|false`*

If this attribute is set to true, PHPMailer uses HTML instead of plaintext. You can embed pretty pictures with HTML, but not all mail clients want to support HTML. See the following attribute if this is a problem.

`$mail->AltBody = `*`text`*

If you set the isHTML attribute to true, you can set the AltBody attribute to a text-only equivalent of the message body.

Adding Attachments

If you want to attach files to messages, use this method:

`$mail->AddAttachment(`*`path, name, encoding, type`*`)`

The parameters are as follows:

path   The full pathname of the file that you want to attach.

name   The new name for the attached file. For example, if the file is called 011100.jpg on your system, but you want it to be called product _sample.jpg, set this parameter to product_sample.jpg. This parameter is optional, but you should always include it in order to make certain that you cause the recipient's client to save the attachment correctly.

encoding   The attachment's encoding. The default is base64, which is perfect for binary attachments.

type   The MIME type of the attachment. The default is application/octet-stream, which is fine for most files. In certain cases, you may want to change this setting. For example, image/jpeg is appropriate for JPEG images. However, unless you know what you're doing, it's best to leave this setting alone and let the recipient's email client figure it out.

To send the message with the attachment, use the normal PHPMailer Send() method. If you need to clear the attachments in an object (for example, if you're iterating through recipients and each has a unique attachment), use this method:

```
$mail->ClearAttachments()
```

Finally, if you have an attachment in a PHP variable, you can use the AddStringAttachment() method to include an attachment. It's just like AddAttachment(), but instead of the path parameter, use a PHP string or variable instead.

What Can Go Wrong?

If you're using the mail() function to send mail, you need to make sure that PHP can actually do so. If it cannot, use SMTP or sendmail instead.

When using STMP to send email, you might get this error message:

```
SMTP Error: The following recipients failed [email@example.com]
```

In most cases, this means that there was an error connecting to the SMTP server. You could have mistyped the SMTP hostname, or the SMTP server might be down. However, the most common case is that the server requires SMTP authentication. Make sure that SMTPAuth is set to true, set the correct username and password for that server, and try again.

It's important to remember that email can be complicated. There are a thousand reasons a given email might not go through to a specific address. The email address could be incorrect, your server could be blacklisted as a spam server, or a server may not like your attachments—and that's just the beginning.

The best way to debug a problem is to start with a plaintext message to an address that is known to work. From there, you can delve into server logs to find particular problems.

#65: Using Email to Verify User Accounts

On sites that have user accounts, some people create accounts just to cause trouble. Perhaps someone will post a bunch of ridiculous comments to your bulletin board or try to overwhelm some other part of your system. A common problem with online stores is that someone may place an order and use a fake email address because he or she doesn't want to be spammed, making it difficult for you to reach that person if you need to ask a question about the order.

One fairly effective way to verify that your users are real is to force them to validate an email address. When you first create the user account, keep it disabled until the user clicks on a verification link in an email message. Accessing the link activates the account.

This section illustrates a system that keeps track of new users who haven't yet activated their accounts. When a user tries to log in to your system, you can first check to see if the account hasn't been activated. You need the following components:

- A MySQL database
- A pending_logins table with two fields: a login and a key. You can create this table with the following SQL (we're using a field called ukey because *key* is a reserved keyword):

```
CREATE TABLE pending_logins (
    'login' varchar(32), 'ukey' varchar(32),
    PRIMARY KEY ('login'),
    INDEX (ukey));
```

- PHPMailer, already installed and in the phpmailer directory

There are three functions in all: a verification generator, an activator, and a verifier. All of these functions assume that you have already validated the login name as a MySQL-safe string, because they always appear inside other code. Let's first look at the verification-generator function. You need to place a call into your account-generation code to generate a key for unlocking the account and then send that key to the user's email address. The first part generates a random 32-character string of lowercase letters to serve as a key to unlock the account:

```
function make_verification($login, $email, $db) {
    /* Generate an account verification link and send it to the user. */

    /* Generate key. */
    $key = ""; $i = 0;
    while ($i < 32) {
        $key .= chr(rand(97, 122));
        $i++;
    }
```

Next we place the key in the pending_logins table. Because the login is the primary key, and therefore multiple rows per login are not allowed, we make sure that there are no preexisting rows; then we insert the data into the table:

```
/* Place the key in the table; first delete any preexisting key. */
    $query = "DELETE FROM pending_logins WHERE login = '$login'";
    mysql_query($query, $db);
    $query = "INSERT INTO pending_logins (login, ukey) VALUES ('$login',
'$key')";
    mysql_query($query, $db);
    if (mysql_error($db)) {
        print "Key generation error.";
        return false;
    }
```

Now we need to generate the URL that the user must visit to activate the account. Obviously, you'll need to change this to your own server name and activation script, but make sure that you send the key as a parameter somewhere:

```
/* Activation URL */
    $url = "http://accounts.example.com/activate.php?k=$key";
```

All that's left to do is send the email to the user. You'll likely want to customize this part as well.

```
include_once("phpmailer/class.phpmailer.php");
    $mail = new PHPMailer;
    $mail->ClearAddresses();
    $mail->AddAddress($email, $login);
    $mail->From = 'generator@example.com';
    $mail->FromName = 'Account Generator';
    $mail->Subject = 'Account verification';
    $mail->Body = "To activate your account, please click
on the account generation URL below:

$url

";
    if ($mail->Send()) {
        print "Verification message sent.";
    } else {
        print $mail->ErrorInfo;
        return false;
    }
    return true;
}
```

To use this function, call it as follows (*db* is a MySQL database handle that you have opened previously). It returns true if the account was placed in the `pending_logins` table and PHPMailer was able to send the activation message:

```
make_verification(login, email_address, db)
```

Now that we have the verification part out of the way, the next part is a function to activate an account when the user clicks on the link. The first thing to do is to sanitize the key sent to us in case the user goofed up or someone is trying to break in. Because the generator used only lowercase characters, we'll just throw out anything that doesn't fit:

```
function activate_account($key, $db) {
    /* Activate an account based on a key. */

    /* Clean up the key if necessary. */
    $key = preg_replace("/[^a-z]/", "", $key);
```

Now we see if the key is bogus or not. If it's not even in the `pending_logins` table, there's nothing to do, and we return false to indicate that we didn't do anything:

```
    $query = "SELECT login FROM pending_logins WHERE ukey = '$key'";
    $c = mysql_query($query, $db);
    if (mysql_num_rows($c) != 1) {
        return false;
    }
```

If we get this far, we know that the key exists in the table, so all we need to do is remove that row to activate the login. Notice that we don't even need to know what the login name is.

```
    $query = "DELETE FROM pending_logins WHERE ukey = '$key'";
    mysql_query($query, $db);
    if (mysql_error($db)) {
        return false;
    }
    return true;
}
```

To use this function, call it as follows:

```
activate_account($_REQUEST["k"], db)
```

The final piece is a function that you need to place inside your user login code to determine whether the account is active or not. If an account has not been activated, it has a row in the pending_logins table. Therefore, you need only look up a username in that table:

```
function is_active($login, $db) {
    /* See if an account has been activated. */
    $query = "SELECT count(*) AS c FROM pending_logins WHERE login =
'$login'";
    $c = mysql_query($query, $db);
    if (mysql_error($db)) {
        return false;
    }
    $r = mysql_fetch_array($c);
    if (intval($r["c"]) > 0) {
        return false;
    }
    return true;
}
```

There are many things you may need to do to this system to make it fit in with your site. For example, you can add a timestamp field to the table so that you can cull inactive accounts that are never verified. There may be many other reasons to deactivate an account; in that case, you need to store a reason for deactivation in the table. You may even want to include the activation key in the main login table. The activation mechanism illustrated here is specifically meant to plug into foreign login systems with minimal pain.

10

WORKING WITH IMAGES

This chapter shows you how to create and manipulate images such as GIFs and JPEGs. You won't be able to write scripts for heavy-duty image manipulation or processing such as online character recognition (your webserver limits the amount of computation that one script can do), but there are many small image operations that are very handy when developing a website.

#66: Creating a CAPTCHA (Security) Image

Because many examples in this book use cURL to connect to and interact with websites, you know how easy it is to automate interactions with websites. You also know that if you have a site feature that you want no one but a real human to work with, you need to protect it. Otherwise, you may (at the very least) find your site completely overrun by spam comments. One way around this problem is to dynamically draw an image containing text that a user must type in order to post a comment (or perform some other human-only action, such as voting or rating). If you get the correct text from the user, the user is probably human.

This sort of test is named *CAPTCHA*, for *Completely Automated Public Turing Test to Tell Computers and Humans Apart.* It has two drawbacks. First, if you're blind, you can't read the text from the CAPTCHA image. Visually impaired people can use the Internet with the help of voice software to read the pages aloud, but this software can't interpret images without the descriptive alt attribute. A CAPTCHA locks out these users.

Furthermore, a CAPTCHA doesn't always work. Spammers are always looking for ways around your roadblocks. One of the more creative ways is linking the CAPTCHA image to a spammer-owned porn site with a label of *INPUT THIS PHRASE AND SEE NAKED PEOPLE!* Then some lonely guy inputs the password, which is then passed back to your site.

With these two shortcomings in mind, you should use CAPTCHAs sparingly and weigh them against alternatives such as the Akismet scanner. The CAPTCHA presented here is simple (see Figure 10-1 for a screenshot), but it is effective. To use it, your PHP must have the GD graphics library with Freetype support. To see if you have GD support, use phpinfo() as described in "#8: Revealing All of PHP's Settings" on page 21. The output contains a section on GD with Freetype information if everything is okay. If the section is not there, rebuild PHP as described in "#18: Adding Extensions to PHP" on page 27.

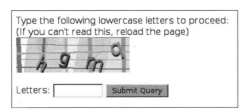

Figure 10-1: A CAPTCHA interface

You also need one or more fonts in the same directory as the script. It's best to go with fonts that are at least halfway readable.

There are two pieces to this system:

1. The main part is a script that creates CAPTCHA images. These images have irregular backgrounds, with strange swaths of color and lines running both horizontally and vertically. Then the script picks a passphrase, stores it in the $_SESSION['tt_pass'] variable, and draws each letter in the passphrase differently. Finally, it sends the image output.

2. The second piece is a script to compare a CAPTCHA form's input with the $_SESSION['tt_pass'] variable. The script here is a simple demonstration, but because the image-generator script does most of the work, you won't need to do much to make it fit your own needs.

Let's start with the image generator. The first step is to set several config-uration variables for the length of the passphrase, the image size, and the place to look for fonts:

```php
<?php
/* captcha_image.php */

/* Passphrase length */
$pass_length = 4;

/* Image dimensions */
$width = 200;
$height = 60;

/* TTF font path */
$font_path = dirname(__FILE__);
```

Now let's create the passphrase. Unlike most passwords, this doesn't need to be particularly challenging: There's no need to annoy your users more than you have to.

```php
session_start();

/* Create a passphrase. */
$passwd = "";
$i = 0;
while ($i < $pass_length) {
    $passwd .= chr(rand(97, 122));
    $i++;
}
```

We'll put the passphrase in a session variable. Therefore, it never appears in any pages in any form of encoding. This avoids the need to come up with an encoding that someone will just break.

```php
/* Store passphrase. */
$_SESSION["tt_pass"] = $passwd;
```

Before drawing anything, we want to make sure that we have some fonts to use for the image. This code creates a list of fonts in the current directory. If you'd like to make this part faster, you can set the $fonts array to a set of TrueType font filenames:

```php
/* Get a list of available fonts. */
$fonts = array();

if ($handle = opendir($font_path)) {
    while (false !== ($file = readdir($handle))) {
        /* Look for TTF fonts. */
        if (substr(strtolower($file), -4, 4) == '.ttf') {
            $fonts[] = $font_path . '/' . $file;
```

```
        }
    }
}

if (count($fonts) < 1)  {
    die("No fonts found!");
}
```

The client has to know what kind of image you're sending. This script creates a JPEG image, so it sends that MIME type. In addition, we don't want the browser to cache the image, so we'll send several cache-invalidating headers:

```
/* Image header */
header("Content-Type: image/jpeg");
/* Invalidate cache. */
header("Expires: Mon, 01 Jul 1998 05:00:00 GMT");
header("Last-Modified: " . gmdate("D, d M Y H:i:s") . " GMT");
header("Cache-Control: no-store, no-cache, must-revalidate");
header("Cache-Control: post-check=0, pre-check=0", false);
header("Pragma: no-cache");
```

With all of the preparatory work complete, we can now start creating the image. GD functions begin with an `image` prefix. To initialize a color image canvas, use `imagecreatetruecolor()`.

```
/* Create image. */
$img = imagecreatetruecolor($width, $height);
```

The first thing we'll draw is a rectangle to cover the entire background. To draw anything, you need to allocate a color in the image with `imagecreatetruecolor()`. The second, third, and fourth parameters to this function are the red, green, and blue values of the color, respectively. The value is an integer between 0 and 255, with 0 being the darkest and 255 being the lightest. The following statement creates a random pastel color:

```
/* Fill background with a random shade of pastel. */
$bg = imagecolorallocate($img, rand(210,255), rand(210,255), rand(210,255));
```

Now let's draw that rectangle with the `imagefilledrectangle()` function. The rectangle is parallel to the image axes, so you can define it by two points: (0, 0) and ($width, $height):

```
imagefilledrectangle($img, 0, 0, $width, $height, $bg);
```

To convolute the background some more, we'll draw several vertically oriented polygons across the canvas. The following loop creates the polygons with the `imagefilledpolygon()` function. This is different than drawing a rectangle because a polygon can have three or more sides in any orientation, so you need to provide an array of points as a parameter (here, $poly_points) instead of two sets of coordinates.

Try not to get sucked into the details of this loop. It is not a terribly important part of this script.

```
/* Make the background jaggedy by creating different-colored
   four-cornered polygons to cover the background area. */

/* Create swaths between 10 and 30 pixels wide across the image. */
$right = rand(10, 30);
$left = 0;
while ($left < $width) {
    $poly_points = array(
        $left, 0,                              /* Upper left */
        $right, 0,                             /* Upper right */
        rand($right-25, $right+25), $height,   /* Lower right */
        rand($left-15, $left+15), $height);    /* Lower left */

    /* Create the polygon, using four points from the array. */
    $c = imagecolorallocate($img, rand(210,255), rand(210,255), rand(210,255));
    imagefilledpolygon($img, $poly_points, 4, $c);

    /* Advance to the right edge. */
    $random_amount = rand(10, 30);
    $left += $random_amount;
    $right += $random_amount;
}
```

To further thwart those who might use OCR software to try to break this system, let's draw some random horizontal and vertical lines across the screen. To mix it up even more, we'll define a different color range for the lines for each image. By choosing random lower and upper bounds for the colors, the lines may or may not vary in intensity and will vary in consistency from image to image.

```
/* Choose base value range for vertical and horizontal lines. */
$c_min = rand(120, 185);
$c_max = rand(195, 280);
```

To draw the vertical lines, start at the left side and pick a thickness and a slight offset to tilt the line. Then pick a color (using the preceding bounds), draw the line as a polygon, and advance to the right by yet another random amount:

```
/* Draw random vertical lines across the width. */
$left = 0;
while ($left < $width) {
    $right = $left + rand(3, 7);
    $offset = rand(-3, 3);                     /* Offset for angle */

    $line_points = array(
        $left, 0,                              /* Upper left */
        $right, 0,                             /* Upper right */
```

```
                $right + $offset, $height,                    /* Lower right */
                $left + $offset, $height);                    /* Lower left */

        $pc = imagecolorallocate($img, rand($c_min, $c_max),
                                       rand($c_min, $c_max),
                                       rand($c_min, $c_max));
        imagefilledpolygon($img, $line_points, 4, $pc);

        /* Advance to the right. */
        $left += rand(20, 60);
    }
```

Use the same procedure to create the horizontal lines:

```
/* Create random horizontal lines across the height. */
$top = 0;
while ($top < $height) {
    $bottom = $top + rand(1, 4);
    $offset = rand(-6, 6);                         /* Offset for angle */

    $line_points = array(
        0, $top,                                   /* Upper left */
        0, $bottom,                                /* Lower left */
        $width, $bottom + $offset,                 /* Lower right */
        $width, $top + $offset);                   /* Upper right */
    $pc = imagecolorallocate($img, rand($c_min, $c_max),
                                   rand($c_min, $c_max),
                                   rand($c_min, $c_max));
    imagefilledpolygon($img, $line_points, 4, $pc);
    $top += rand(8, 15);
}
```

We're finally ready for the passphrase characters. Before drawing, determine roughly how far apart you want the letters to appear, and then set a variable to the leftmost character position:

```
/* Determine character spacing. */
$spacing = $width / (strlen($passwd)+2);

/* Initial x coordinate */
$x = $spacing;
```

Now, iterate through the characters and pick a slightly different offset, angle, size, and font each time:

```
/* Draw each character. */
for ($i = 0; $i < strlen($passwd); $i++) {
    $letter = $passwd[$i];
    $size = rand($height/3, $height/2);
    $rotation = rand(-30, 30);
```

```
/* Random y position with room for character descenders */
$y = rand($height * .90, $height - $size - 4);

/* Pick a random font. */
$font = $fonts[array_rand($fonts)];
```

The letters will be very difficult to read without some sort of outlining. You can create a shadow color by dividing the original color values by 3:

```
/* Pick a color for the letter. */
$r = rand(100, 255); $g = rand(100, 255); $b = rand(100, 255);

/* Create letter and shadow colors. */
$color = imagecolorallocate($img, $r, $g, $b);
$shadow = imagecolorallocate($img, $r/3, $g/3, $b/3);
```

Use imagettftext() to draw the shadow and then the letter, and advance to the next character:

```
/* Draw shadow, then letter. */
imagettftext($img, $size, $rotation, $x, $y, $shadow, $font, $letter);
imagettftext($img, $size, $rotation, $x-1, $y-3, $color, $font, $letter);

/* Advance across the canvas. */
$x += rand($spacing, $spacing * 1.5);
}
```

Once this loop is complete, you're ready to send the image to the client. Use imagejpeg() to do so, and then deallocate its memory with imagedestroy():

```
imagejpeg($img);         /* Send image output. */
imagedestroy($img);      /* Free image memory. */

?>
```

The other piece of the CAPTCHA system is a small piece of code to display the form, embed an image with the preceding script, and verify that the form input is the passphrase the image generator created. Because the image script does all of the hard work, you'll be able to figure out the following without comment:

```
<?php

session_start();

/* Look for a submitted password. */
if ($_REQUEST["tt_pass"]) {
    if ($_REQUEST["tt_pass"] == $_SESSION["tt_pass"]) {
        echo "passphrase correct.";
    } else {
```

```
        echo "passphrase incorrect.";
    }
    exit(0);
}

/* By default, send the form. */

print '<form action="' . $_SERVER['PHP_SELF'] . '" method="post">';
?>

Type the following lowercase letters to proceed:<br />
(If you can't read this, reload the page)<br />
<img src="captcha_image.php"><br /><br />
Letters: <input name="tt_pass" type="text" size="10" maxlength="10">
<input type="submit">
</form>
```

Obviously, you'll need to incorporate this script into your code more tightly, but one of the best aspects of this system is that it's relatively self-contained. There are several things you could do to tighten it up a little, such as deleting the stored passphrase once it is verified (so it can be used only once). But if you find yourself needing much more, you might have a larger problem that you need to solve with a login system.

#67: Creating Thumbnail Images

When you allow users to upload images to your site (see "#54: Uploading Images to a Directory" on page 97), you often need a small preview image (called a *thumbnail*) for inclusion on larger pages and image gallery browsing. This section shows you a function called mkthumb() that creates thumbnails with the help of GD. To use the function, you need the following:

- A PHP-writable directory for writing the thumbnails (if you don't know how to make a directory writable, see "File Permissions" on page 91)
- The GD library

The mkthumb() function takes two parameters: the name of the input image file and the desired name of the thumbnail. You need to independently verify that the image file exists and has a .jpg, .gif, or .png extension. If you haven't done that already, check out "#54: Uploading Images to a Directory" on page 97. With all that out of the way, start by defining default values for the maximum thumbnail width and height (for this function, these dimensions must be equal):

```
<?php
function mkthumb($filename, $thumbname) {
    /* Generate an image thumbnail. */
    $thumb_width = 125;
    $thumb_height = $thumb_width;
```

Now load the image into memory based on the file extension. The GD imagecreatefrom*format*() functions return an image resource handle. One thing you'll notice right away is that there is no error checking here, primarily because mkthumb() assumes that you've taken care of the prerequisites. If you need error checking, check $src_image afterward to see if it exists.

```
if (preg_match('/\.gif$/i', $filename)) {
    $src_image = imagecreatefromgif($filename);
} else if (preg_match('/\.png$/i', $filename)) {
    $src_image = imagecreatefrompng($filename);
} else {
    /* Assume JPEG by default. */
    $src_image = imagecreatefromjpeg($filename);
}
```

Now extract the pixel width and height from the image with the imagesx() and imagesy() functions:

```
$width = imagesx($src_image);
$height = imagesy($src_image);
```

You resize the image only when the original image is larger than the maximum thumbnail dimensions, so check to see if this is the case:

```
if (($height > $thumb_height) || ($width > $thumb_width)) {
```

When resizing an image, you need to know the final image dimensions in pixels. You can't use the maximum thumbnail height and width, because the original image is probably not square. If you try to shoehorn a non-square rectangle into a square, you will end up with a distorted image. To solve this problem, find the longest side of the original image, and then create a scaling ratio based on the ratio between length of the longest side and the length of the thumbnail side:

```
/* Create a thumbnail. */
if ($width > $height) {
    $ratio = $thumb_width / $width;
} else {
    $ratio = $thumb_height / $height;
}
```

WARNING *The reason the maximum thumbnail dimensions are square in this function is that the preceding logic errs for general rectangles. If you try to put a 200 × 400 image into a 100 × 400 thumbnail profile, $ratio is 1, and you end up with a 200 × 400 thumbnail (see the following code). That size is larger than the desired maximum thumbnail size. Fixing this problem is not difficult, but it is left as an exercise to the reader.*

Use the ratio to find the exact thumbnail dimensions in pixels, and create a new image resource handle for the resized image:

```
$new_width = round($width * $ratio);
$new_height = round($height * $ratio);
$dest_image = ImageCreateTrueColor($new_width, $new_height);
```

Now you can perform the resizing with imagecopyresampled():

```
imagecopyresampled($dest_image, $src_image, 0, 0, 0, 0,
                   $new_width, $new_height, $width, $height);
```

You can then free the memory for the original image:

```
imagedestroy($src_image);
```

At this point, $dest_image is an image resource containing the resized image, ready for output. But what if we didn't need to resize? The code falls through to the following else clause, which says that it's fine to assign $dest_image to the original image handle:

```
} else {
    /* Image is already small enough; just output. */
    $dest_image = $src_image;
}
```

Because we now know that $dest_image is ready for output, we can write it to a file and clean up:

```
imagejpeg($dest_image, $thumbname);
imagedestroy($dest_image);
}

?>
```

Here's a very simple example script that uses the `mkthumb()` function:

```php
<?php
include("mkthumb.inc");
$upfile = $_FILES["upfile"]["tmp_name"];
$fn = $_FILES["upfile"]["name"];
$thumb_filename = "thumbs/$fn";

if ($upfile) {
    mkthumb($upfile, $thumb_filename);
    print "<img src=\"$thumb_filename\" />";
} else { ?>
    <form action="thumb.php" enctype="multipart/form-data" method="post">
    Upload an image:<br />
    <input name="upfile" type="file" /><br />
    <input name="Submit" type="submit" value="Upload Image" />
    <?
}
?>
```

Obviously, this script makes a *lot* of assumptions, and you'd never want to use it for general users. Again, use "#54: Uploading Images to a Directory" on page 97 for a full-blown image uploader.

There are several optimizations that you can do for `mkthumb()` in order to suit your particular needs. For example, JPEG is a lossy format. If you make a thumbnail of a cartoon-style GIF or PNG, the resulting thumbnail will be of poor quality. To fix this problem, you may elect to write in the PNG format with the `imagepng()` function instead of `imagejpeg()`. You could also try to get tricky and resize into the image's original format. However, this may backfire on you, because GIF images have a limited color map, and when you resize an image, the color map tends to change.

Overall, though, beware of trying to be *too* tricky with PHP image manipulation. PHP is typically used on demand, so you have little time for fancy operations. In addition to the user getting impatient, the webserver won't let a script run for very long.

11

USING cURL TO INTERACT WITH WEB SERVICES

The Internet holds a lot of very useful data: UPS can tell you exactly how much it costs to ship a five-pound package from Baton Rouge, Louisiana, to Hartford, Connecticut. Authorize.net can tell you whether a customer has enough credit left on his debit card to buy a $60 book from your site. But in each case, you need to know how to ask for the information.

In order to find the information, the first thing you need is the cURL PHP library to handle the connection between your webserver and other webservers. The idea is to make your scripts act like clients, similar to the way web browsers work. You can ask cURL to do anything from retrieving the HTML from a web page to directly accessing an XML-based web service. There are three basic ways to access data:

- Download the site's web page to pick through the HTML. Chapter 5 contained an example: "#41: Creating a Screen Scraper" on page 75.

- Post query parameters to a website, and pick through the results.
- Use an XML-based web service to access data, and use an XML parser to access the results. You'll encounter several different access protocols, such as SOAP (Simple Object Access Protocol) and REST (REpresentational State Transfer; usually this is just a fancy term for sending POST or GET parameters). Don't expect much consistency. Even two sites that provide the same type of data will probably have completely different output formats and access methods.

You'll also need a subset of the following libraries, depending on what you need to do:

1. cURL (the library and the PHP extension). See "#18: Adding Extensions to PHP" on page 27 if you do not have the extension.
2. OpenSSL for accessing secure sites.
3. XML for parsing data from web services. Most PHP servers include this by default.

#68: Connecting to Other Websites

To illustrate how the PHP cURL functions work, let's look at how to make a connection to a web page and retrieve its data. First, create a cURL connection handle with the curl_init() function:

```
$c = curl_init();
```

Now use the curl_setopt() function to specify the connection settings. The most important setting is the target URL. Call the function as follows, with CURLOPT_URL as the option name and the last argument the desired URL:

```
curl_setopt($c, CURLOPT_URL, "http://www.google.com/");
```

By default, cURL enables certain features that are either not useful or get in the way of normal page processing. One of these features is including the HTTP header with the output. You can turn it off as follows:

```
curl_setopt($c, CURLOPT_HEADER, false);
```

Similarly, cURL automatically prints the accessed page instead of returning it as a string. You need a string if you intend to analyze the page somehow, so use the CURLOPT_RETURNTRANSFER option to say that you want the output as a string:

```
curl_setopt($c, CURLOPT_RETURNTRANSFER, true);
```

You're now ready to access the page with the curl_exec() function:

```
$page_data = curl_exec($c);
```

At this point, cURL accesses the page and returns the page data, which PHP assigns to $page_data. Finally, clean up after the connection with curl_close():

```
curl_close($c);
```

This is a good start; you can now access web data via the GET method. But what if you need to use the POST method to submit form data? In this case, you need to set more options with curl_setopt(). Let's build a function called retrieve_page() that can access pages with the GET or POST methods.

The function takes two arguments: a URL to access and an optional array of POST parameters (the array has parameter names as keys and the parameter values as its values). If it doesn't receive this second argument, the function uses the GET method. The first part of the function builds a query string from the parameter array in the form parm1=value1&parm2=value2[...], much like it would appear in a GET query, except that it does not include the leading question mark. Fortunately, PHP has a built-in http_build_query() function to create a query string from an array, so all we really need to do is verify the parameter array:

```
function retrieve_page($url, $post_parameters = null) {
    /* Connects to a site using POST or GET; fetches data */
    $query_string = null;
    if (!is_null($post_parameters)) {
        if (!is_array($post_parameters)) {
            die("POST parameters not in array format");
        }
        /* Build query string. */
        $query_string = http_build_query($post_parameters);
    }
}
```

Now it's time to set up the cURL connection handle. If there is a query string at this point, we know that we're using the POST method, so we configure the connection in that manner and use the query string as the POST data:

```
$ch = curl_init();

if ($query_string) {
    curl_setopt($ch, CURLOPT_POST, true);
    curl_setopt($ch, CURLOPT_POSTFIELDS, $query_string);
}
```

From this point on, we configure the connection as we did before, execute the query, and return the data:

```
curl_setopt($ch, CURLOPT_URL, $url);
curl_setopt($ch, CURLOPT_HEADER, false);
curl_setopt($ch, CURLOPT_RETURNTRANSFER, true);
$return_data = curl_exec($ch);
curl_close($ch);
```

```
        return $return_data;
}
```

Here's an example of how to use this function for searching Yahoo!:

```
print retrieve_page("http://search.yahoo.com/search", array("p" => "beans"));
```

This function works for most casual client-access needs. From here on, we'll illustrate how to satisfy the myriad extra requirements of some websites and services.

#69: Using Cookies

If your application requires that you log in to a server that has cookie-based authentication, then you need to enable a cookie collection system in cURL. The idea is that when you access a page, cURL stores the cookies it receives in a file (called the *cookie jar*), and upon subsequent accesses, you want cURL to check that file for any cookies that it should send to the server.

Typically, you need to add two configuration lines: the first to set the write location and the second to set the read location:

```
curl_setopt(c, CURLOPT_COOKIEJAR, 'cookiejar');
curl_setopt(c, CURLOPT_COOKIEFILE, 'cookiejar');
```

Here, *c* is a cURL connection handle, and *cookiejar* is a PHP-writable file.
The biggest problem with this scheme is that it does not work with parallel connections; if you have more than one process using the same cookie jar, then they'll all have the same session, trample each other, or worse. You can get around this by inserting the PHP process ID (use getmypid()) into the cookie jar filename. However, if you do so, make sure that you clean up by removing the cookie jar file when you're finished, or you will have a really big collection of cookie jars on your hands that may confuse subsequent processes.

#70: Transforming XML into a Usable Form

XML (eXtensible Markup Language) is one of the most popular products of the markup language fad. It's designed to provide standard interchange formats for any kind of data. Though XML is bloated and tremendously inefficient, most web services now use XML in their output, and some services even require XML as input. Therefore, you likely will need to deal with it at some point.

The best way to get started with XML is to parse a piece of it—that is, verify that the data is valid XML and examine the data. You'd think that with all of the hype that accompanied the introduction of XML, someone would have come up with an easy way to work with it. Unfortunately, for many years, accessing XML data was ruthlessly complicated; as a result, a myriad of parsing systems appeared, such as DOM and SAX. If you've ever been confused by the 27,000 different XML extensions available in PHP, you now know why.

The good news is that somewhere along the way, people realized that most of the time they were just parsing the XML data into a tree composed of a bunch of nested arrays, so that programmers could use normal data-access tools such as iterators and indexes. A new generation of parsers appeared to serve this purpose; PHP 5 includes such an extension, called *SimpleXML*.

Here's some sample XML to get us started with SimpleXML:

```
<?xml version="1.0" encoding="utf-8"?>
<preaching>
 <sins>
   <sin type="deadly">gluttony</sin>
   <sin type="minor">bad puns</sin>
   <sin type="required">flatulence</sin>
 </sins>
</preaching>
```

This XML contains nested nodes, data, and attributes, so it covers most of what you'll ever encounter. To parse it with SimpleXML, load the data into a string and create a `SimpleXMLElement` object from the string:

```
$xs = file_get_contents("test.xml");
$data = new SimpleXMLElement($xs);
```

NOTE   *You can use `simplexml_load_file()` to create the object from a file instead of using this two-step process.*

If you don't get an overly verbose error message, the XML is now in the $data object. To look at the first sin in the <sins> node, use a combination of object- and array-access syntax:

```
print $data->sins->sin[0];
```

The output is gluttony; if you wanted to access the bad puns node, you'd look at $data->sins->sin[1]. If you omit the array index ($data->sins->sin), you'll get the first element of the array; this is handy if you know that there is a single element.

You can look at a node's attributes using array indexes as well, except that this time the indexes are keys instead of numbers. For example, to find out what type of sin bad puns is, use the following:

```
print $data->sins->sin[1]["type"];
```

Probably the best thing about the array syntax is that you iterate over nodes.

Here's how to print out all of the sins in our sample:

```
foreach ($data->sins->sin as $sin) {
    print $sin . " : " . $sin["type"];
    print "<br />";
}
```

As you have probably noticed, it's possible to get confused between attributes and child nodes with this syntax, but in general it's not too bad. You can even use print_r() to print the whole mess if you ever get lost. The output looks like this:

```
SimpleXMLElement Object
(
    [sins] => SimpleXMLElement Object
        (
            [sin] => Array
                (
                    [0] => gluttony
                    [1] => bad puns
                    [2] => flatulence
                )
        )
)
```

There's a lot more to SimpleXML, including the ability to create and modify XML, but this is what you need to know to get started with web services. In the next few sections, we'll look at a few real-world applications.

#71: Using Mapping Web Services

At this point, you know how to access a URL and how to parse XML, so now it's time to put the two together. Let's look at the Yahoo! geocoding service as a simple example. The API is a REST service that you can access through GET parameters. Assuming that you have the retrieve_page() function from "#68: Connecting to Other Websites" on page 142, here's how to get information for a prominent address in Washington, D.C.

```
$qs = http_build_query(array(
    "appid"     => "YahooDemo",
    "street"    => "1600 Pennsylvania Avenue NW",
    "city"      => "Washington",
    "state"     => "DC",
    "zip"       => "20006",
));
$page = retrieve_page("http://local.yahooapis.com/MapsService/V1/geocode?$qs");
```

Ideally, you want to replace YahooDemo with your Yahoo!-supplied application ID, although you can leave it as is if you don't plan to use this application in production or repeatedly.

After this code runs, $page contains the following XML result:

```
<?xml version="1.0"?>
<ResultSet xmlns:xsi="http://www.w3.org/2001/XMLSchema-instance" xmlns="urn
:yahoo:maps" xsi:schemaLocation="urn:yahoo:maps http://api.local.yahoo.com/
MapsService/V1/GeocodeResponse.xsd">
    <Result precision="address">
        <Latitude>38.898563</Latitude>
        <Longitude>-77.037223</Longitude>
        <Address>1600 PENNSYLVANIA AVE NW</Address>
        <City>WASHINGTON</City>
        <State>DC</State>
        <Zip>20006</Zip>
        <Country>US</Country>
    </Result>
</ResultSet>
```

So, to extract the latitude and longitude of the address, use the following PHP code:

```
$data = new SimpleXMLElement($page);
$lat1 = $data->Result->Latitude[0];
$lon1 = $data->Result->Longitude[0];
```

If all you wanted were the latitude and longitude of an address, you've now successfully used the web service. But let's do something a little more fun. First, assume that the script is called mapdemo.php, run from the following form:

```
<form action="mapdemo.php">
Street: <input type="text" name="street" /><br />
City: <input type="text" name="city" /><br />
State: <input type="text" name="state" /><br />
<input type="submit" /><br>
</form>
```

Add the following to mapdemo.php in order to extract a second geolocation from the arbitrary address entered in the preceding form:

```
$qs = http_build_query(array(
    "appid"     => "YahooDemo",
    "street"    => $_REQUEST["street"],
    "city"      => $_REQUEST["city"],
    "state"     => $_REQUEST["state"],
));
```

```
$page = retrieve_page("http://local.yahooapis.com/MapsService/V1/
geocode?$qs");
$data = new SimpleXMLElement($page);
$lat2 = $data->Result->Latitude[0];
$lon2 = $data->Result->Longitude[0];
```

Now let's draw something on the browser using the Google Maps API but based on the data that we got from the Yahoo! service. Start by closing the PHP block and setting up a Google map with this HTML and JavaScript (replace *your_key_here* with your Google Maps API key). If you don't know JavaScript, don't worry too much about this part, because it's very standard:

```
?>
<!DOCTYPE html "-//W3C//DTD XHTML 1.0 Strict//EN"
  "http://www.w3.org/TR/xhtml1/DTD/xhtml1-strict.dtd">
<html xmlns="http://www.w3.org/1999/xhtml">
  <head>
    <meta http-equiv="content-type" content="text/html; charset=utf-8"/>
    <title>Map Example</title>
    <script src="http://maps.google.com/
maps?file=api&amp;v=2&amp;key=your_key_here"
            type="text/javascript"></script>
    <script type="text/javascript">

    function initialize() {
      if (GBrowserIsCompatible()) {
        var map = new GMap2(document.getElementById("map_canvas"));
```

Now, create points in the Google map for the two geolocations that you extracted earlier, and center the map on the first point (you must center the map before performing any operations):

```
        var latlon1 = new GLatLng(<?php print "$lat1, $lon1"; ?>);
        var latlon2 = new GLatLng(<?php print "$lat2, $lon2"; ?>);
        map.setCenter(latlon1);
```

Place markers on the map where the points lie:

```
        map.addOverlay(new GMarker(latlon1));
        map.addOverlay(new GMarker(latlon2));
```

Draw a line between the points:

```
        var line = new GPolyline([latlon1, latlon2], "#3333aa", 5);
        map.addOverlay(line);
```

Now, recenter and rezoom the map so that the entire line is in full view:

```
        var bounds = line.getBounds();
        level = map.getBoundsZoomLevel(bounds);
        map.setCenter(bounds.getCenter(), level);
```

Finally, add a user control panel (for zooming and panning), and wrap up with the HTML to display the map:

```
      map.addControl(new GLargeMapControl());
    }
  }

  </script>
</head>
<body onload="initialize()" onunload="GUnload()">
  <div id="map_canvas" style="width: 500px; height: 300px"></div>
</body>
</html>
```

Now you have a simple application that draws a line on a Google map between the White House and the address you choose. By itself, this script is a bit of a toy (especially because you can get the geolocation code from Google instead of Yahoo!), but you can probably imagine many different ways it can serve as a starting point for real applications.

We could go on and on with web services, showing you how to authorize credit cards and get shipping quotes, but all of that is busy work at this point—you gather the data from the client, package it for the server, send the request, and check the results. For much of this, you can even find PHP client code to do the work for you. However, one topic we have not yet discussed is SOAP, and this protocol is very important in many web services.

#72: Using PHP and SOAP to Request Data from Amazon.com

Simple Object Access Protocol (SOAP) is a full-blown web service standard that, like anything with *simple* in the name, is far from simple. The idea is to place all of the details concerning the input and output of a web service into a Web Services Description Language (WSDL) document, so that you can automatically generate a programming interface and call a web service just as you would a method or function. You don't have to mess around with cURL, building queries, or any of that stuff—just create an object with your request, tell PHP to create the interface, call the method, and you get an object containing your goodies. In fact, when everything works the way it should, it *is* as easy as that, and the script in this section shows you how to get started.

PHP 5 includes a collection of built-in SOAP classes, including the SoapClient class that we'll see soon. However, the classes typically aren't built in by default. To use it, you need to include the --enable-soap parameter when configuring and building PHP (refer back to Chapter 2 for more details on this process).

Our example is based on the Associates Web Service that Amazon.com offers to help you sell its goods from your website. All you need to do is apply for an access key ID, and then you can access it for free (at a rate of one request per second). Start by creating a `SoapClient` instance with the location of the WSDL document:

```php
<?php
$client = new SoapClient("http://webservices.amazon.com/AWSECommerceService/
AWSECommerceService.wsdl");
```

Now you need to set up an object for the request you want to send. Set up an object called `$search` containing nodes for your access key ID, the category, and keywords for a search:

```php
$search->AWSAccessKeyId = "your_key_id";
$search->Request->SearchIndex = "Music";
$search->Request->Keywords = "Merle Haggard";
```

To perform the search, run the client's `itemSearch()` method:

```php
$r = $client->itemSearch($search);
```

If everything goes well, the XML results appear in `$r`. You can access this object in much the same way you would a SimpleXML instance:

```php
foreach ($r->Items->Item as $item) {
    $attributes = $item->ItemAttributes;
    if (is_array($attributes->Artist)) {
        $artist = implode($attributes->Artist, ", ");
    } else {
        $artist = $attributes->Artist;
    }
    print "artist: $artist; title: $attributes->Title<br />";
}
?>
```

This is remarkably easy to use if you happen to know how everything works. Unfortunately, most of the time, you won't know how everything works. WSDL files often have no accompanying documentation. So assuming that you know how to read WSDL or you have a browser, you can find all of the methods available to the client, and you will know which parameters the methods expect, but you won't know what the parameters do. Furthermore, even though you will know what the responses from the methods will look like, you won't even know exactly what it is the methods are supposed to do. Part of the reason is that it's hard to be concrete about documentation when you don't know which programming language or SOAP implementation you're dealing with. Moreover, no one *wants* to document it.

Performance is another serious issue. In the preceding example, PHP needs to fetch the WSDL file, parse its XML, and then set up an entirely new class and instance based on the WSDL content. This is exceptionally inefficient, especially considering that you normally just need to send a few short parameters to a service. PHP does cache the WSDL files that it sees (other languages may require you to generate and compile code based on the WSDL, which isn't any better).

The bottom line is that if you plan to run a number of web services queries based on WSDL at once, you either need a lot of hardware or some way to bypass most of this process by constructing SOAP queries by hand.

For these reasons, pure SOAP web services aren't as common as you might think. For example, the Amazon.com SOAP Web Service was added only recently, standing alongside a traditional REST service. Amazon.com documents the REST parameters but tells you to "look at the WSDL" for how to do it in SOAP. Another big company by the name of Google decided to discontinue SOAP support for its web search service. However, SOAP is not going away. In particular, you'll almost certainly need to deal with it whenever you encounter services based on Microsoft .NET.

#73: Building a Web Service

To close out this chapter, let's take a quick look at how to build a REST web service. The idea is similar to almost any other kind of dynamic web page, but rather than worrying about how the page looks, all you need to do is properly construct an object, transform the object to XML, and print the result. After that, everything else is someone else's problem (at least, in theory).

We'll use the data from the example table in the appendix. The web service takes a category parameter (as POST or GET) and returns an XML product listing such as this:

```xml
<?xml version="1.0" encoding="utf-8"?>
<Items>
    <Item>
        <Name>Cowboy Boots</Name>
        <ID>12</ID>
        <Price>19.99</Price>
    </Item>
    <Item>
        <Name>Slippers</Name>
        <ID>17</ID>
        <Price>9.99</Price>
    </Item>
</Items>
```

There are many ways to create XML in PHP, from using the DOM to using the xmlwriter functions. We'll use the SimpleXML class from earlier in this chapter. The first thing to do is initialize the database, tell the client that it is about to receive XML, and verify the category parameter. This is mainly busy work; you've seen plenty of code like this by now (don't worry about printerror(); we'll get to it in a bit):

```php
<?php
$db = mysql_connect("localhost", "username", "passwd");
mysql_select_db("wcphp");

header("Content-type: text/xml");
```

```
$category = $_REQUEST["category"];

if ($category) {
    $results = mysql_query("SELECT DISTINCT category FROM product_info", $db);
    $categories = array();
    while ($row = mysql_fetch_array($results)) {
        $categories[] = $row["category"];
    }
    if (!in_array($category, $categories)) {
        printerror("invalid category");
        exit;
    }
}
```

NOTE   *Technically, you needn't go through all of this work to find out the valid category names, because you could cache them (and you should if you need to use them often).*

Now let's grab the product information from the database:

```
$results = mysql_query("
    SELECT product_name, product_id, price
      FROM product_info
     WHERE category = '$category'", $db);
```

Here's where things start to get a little interesting. To initialize the XML document, we'll create a SimpleXMLElement instance from a preexisting XML document. This can be as complicated or as simple as you like. Our basic XML structure is very simple, so we'll just use an inline string:

```
$doc = new SimpleXMLElement('<?xml version="1.0" encoding="utf-8"?>
<Items></Items>
');
```

Our document is ready to fill out, and the data is at hand in $results, so let's iterate through the rows. The first thing to do is add a new Item child to the Items node with the $doc->addChild() method:

```
while ($product = mysql_fetch_array($results)) {
    $child = $doc->addChild("Item");
```

The first new child is accessible at $doc->Item[0], but it's easier to use the handle that the addChild() method returned. That new child now needs children of its own for the Name, ID, and Price nodes, so again you'll use the addChild() method, but this time from $child instead of $doc. In addition, these new nodes have values, so provide those values as the second parameter:

```
    $child->addChild("Name", $product["product_name"]);
    $child->addChild("ID", $product["product_id"]);
    $child->addChild("Price", $product["price"]);
}
```

After you've run through all of the items, all you need to do is output the XML. Use the $doc->asXML() function, and you're finished:

```
print $doc->asXML();
```

Well, you're not *quite* finished yet. Remember that printerror() function we mentioned earlier? Let's take care of that now. Furthermore, let's assume that the error message is dead simple, so we won't even bother with objects:

```
function printerror($message) {
    $message = htmlentities($message);
    print "<?xml version=\"1.0\" encoding=\"utf-8\"?>
<Error>$message</Error>
";
}
?>
```

This is about all there is to web services. There are plenty of ways to make them more complicated, such as using SOAP and WSDL, but at the end of the day, all that you are doing is gathering data and putting it into the appropriate slots.

12

INTERMEDIATE PROJECTS

This final chapter includes three sets of scripts that implement common features on many content-based websites: a voting system, an electronic card service, and a blog. These are all just starting points. Although they certainly work as presented, to use them in production, you will want to adapt them to your own needs and fit them to your security model.

All of these projects use MySQL to store data. The table structure and queries here are somewhat more complicated than what you've seen so far in the book, but it's not a big leap. Each system has its own set of tables, and you'll see how to create them.

#74: A User Poll

Online polls may not be very useful for empowering the people, but they are great tools for figuring out how you might want to spin your content in order to keep users interested, optimize page views, or irritate as many people as you can. The best part about online polls is that they are extremely easy to implement. The one shown here supports multiple polls, so its questions and answers are not hardcoded.

For a typical online poll, you should not worry much about ballot stuffing, since it rarely matters. To keep most people from voting more than once, we'll use a cookie-based system. This is easy to circumvent, but for most purposes, the stakes are so low that no one cares. If you need something better, use a login system for voter registration.

There are four scripts in the online poll:

vote_form.php	Displays a ballot to the user
vote_process.php	Processes a ballot
vote_tally.php	Shows the poll results
vote_include.php	Connects to the database

There are three database tables. The poll table contains the questions:

```
CREATE TABLE `poll` (
`ID` INT NOT NULL AUTO_INCREMENT ,
`question` MEDIUMTEXT NOT NULL ,
PRIMARY KEY ( `ID` )
) TYPE = MYISAM ;
```

The answers table contains the answers for the questions in the poll table. The ID field is meant for joining with the ID field of the poll table:

```
CREATE TABLE `answer` (
`answer_ID` INT NOT NULL AUTO_INCREMENT ,
`ID` INT NOT NULL ,
`answer` MEDIUMTEXT NOT NULL ,
PRIMARY KEY ( `answer_ID` )
) TYPE = MYISAM ;
```

The vote table contains the votes. The ID and answer_ID fields mirror those of the poll and answer tables.

```
CREATE TABLE `vote` (
`ID` INT NOT NULL ,
`answer_ID` INT NOT NULL ,
INDEX ( `ID` )
) TYPE = MYISAM ;
```

Finally, here are some sample question and answer rows:

```
INSERT INTO poll (question) VALUES ("Would you like a cheeseburger?");
INSERT INTO answer (ID, answer) VALUES (1, "Yes.");
INSERT INTO answer (ID, answer) VALUES (1, "No.");
INSERT INTO answer (ID, answer) VALUES (1, "Maybe.");
```

All of the scripts connect to the database, so it makes sense to put the connection details into a single include file called vote_config.php:

```
<?php
$db = @mysql_connect("localhost", "sql_login", "sql_password") or
    die("Couldn't connect.");
@mysql_select_db("wcphp", $db) or die("Couldn't select database.");
?>
```

Now let's look at the component scripts.

Creating a Ballot Form

The vote_form.php script is very straightforward; pass it a poll ID in the poll parameter, and it displays the ballot. Figure 12-1 shows an example ballot.

Start by loading the database configuration and forcing the poll ID parameter to an integer:

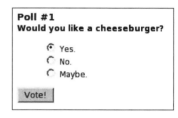

Figure 12-1: A poll ballot

```
<?php
/* Display a vote form. */
require_once("vote_config.php");
$poll = $_GET['poll'];
if (!is_numeric($poll)) {
    die("Invalid poll");
}
```

We can verify that the poll ID is valid and look up the choices to display in one query. The idea is that if no poll matches, no rows come back from the query.

```
/* Look up the poll in the database. */
$sql = "SELECT P.question, A.answer, A.answer_ID
        FROM poll P, answer A
        WHERE P.ID = $poll
          AND A.ID = P.ID";

$result = mysql_query($sql, $db) or die ("mysql error: " . mysql_error());
if (mysql_num_rows($result) == 0) {
    die('Invalid poll.');
}
```

If the poll ID is valid, we have to ensure that the user has not already voted. As previously mentioned, we'll use cookies for this. Assume that if the cookie poll_voted_*id* is present (where *id* is the poll ID), the user has voted, and we should send the user to the poll results.

```
/* If the user has already voted, show the results. */
if ($_COOKIE["poll_voted_$poll"]) {
    header("Location: vote_tally.php?poll=$poll");
    exit;
}
```

If we've gotten this far, it's time to iterate through the list of choices to build the HTML form. This loop places a series of radio button input elements into the $question_list variable:

```
/* Vote form */
$question_list = "";
while($row = mysql_fetch_array($result)) {
    $question = $row['question'];
    $question_list .= '<li><input name="answer" type="radio" value="' .
                      $row['answer_ID'] . '"> ' . $row['answer'] .
                      '</li>';
}
```

There's nothing left to do but print the HTML. We can do most of this in literal mode:

```
?>
<html>
<head></head>
<body>
<span style="font-size: 12px;">
<span style="font-weight: bold; font-size: 14px;">
    Poll #<?php print $poll; ?>
</span><br />
<span style="font-weight: bold"><?php print $question; ?></span>
<form action="vote_process.php" method="post">
<ul style="list-style-type: none;">
<?php print $question_list; ?>
</ul>
<input name="poll" type="hidden" value="<?php print $poll; ?>">
<input name="" type="submit" value="Vote!">
</form>
</span>
</body></html>
```

Notice that the form action is vote_process.php. This is our next script.

Processing the Ballot

The role of vote_process.php is to add a vote to the database if the vote is valid. Start by loading the database configuration and making sure that the poll and answer parameters are numbers.

```php
<?php
require_once("vote_config.php");

$poll = $_POST['poll'];
$answer = $_POST['answer'];
if (!is_numeric($poll) || !is_numeric($answer)) {
    die("Invalid poll or answer");
}
```

We can verify that the poll ID and answer are actually valid by looking for rows that match them in the database. If they check out, a join on the poll and answer tables with these keys will result in exactly one row. However, it's good enough just to see if there are no results to this query:

```php
/* Look up the poll and answer. */
$sql = "SELECT A.answer_ID
        FROM poll P, answer A
        WHERE P.ID = A.ID
        AND P.ID = $poll
        AND A.answer_ID = $answer";

$result = @mysql_query($sql, $db) or die (mysql_error());
if (mysql_num_rows($result) == 0) {
    die('Invalid poll or answer.');
}
```

If we've gotten this far, we can verify that the user has not already voted and insert a vote row into the vote table if everything checks out:

```php
/* Check for prior votes. */
if (!$_COOKIE["poll_voted_$poll"]) {
    /* Insert the vote. */
    $sql = "INSERT INTO `vote` ( `answer_ID` , `ID`)
            VALUES ($answer, $poll);";
    $result = @mysql_query($sql, $db) or
            die ("Couldn't insert: " . mysql_error());
```

If we were successful at inserting the vote, we can set the cookie that indicates that the user has already voted. This cookie will expire in 30 days.

```php
    /* Mark the poll as voted. */
    setcookie("poll_voted_$poll", "1", time() + (60*60*24 * 30));
}
```

Finally, regardless of whether or not the user has previously voted, we send the user to the poll results:

```
/* Redirect to poll results. */
header("Location: vote_tally.php?poll=$poll");
?>
```

Let's look at the results now.

Getting Poll Results

Of course, everyone voting in a poll wants to know the results. We'll use some cheap HTML tricks to display the results as in Figure 12-2.

The vote_tally.php script starts much like our other two, by loading the database configuration and checking for a valid poll ID in the poll parameter:

Poll #1: Would you like a cheeseburger?

Yes.
57.14%
No.
28.57%
Maybe.
14.29%

Total Votes: 7

Figure 12-2: Poll results

```
<?php
/* Display the results of a poll. */
require_once("vote_config.php");

$poll = $_REQUEST['poll'];
if (!is_numeric($poll)) {
    die("Invalid poll");
}
```

When checking for a valid poll ID, we may as well look up the poll question at the same time, because we eventually want to display this information:

```
/* Look up the question. */
$sql = "SELECT question
        FROM poll
        WHERE ID = $poll";
$result = @mysql_query($sql, $db) or die ("mysql error: " . mysql_error());
if (mysql_num_rows($result) != 1) {
    die('Invalid poll.');
}
$row = mysql_fetch_array($result);
$question = $row["question"];
```

Let's find out the total number of votes in order to give some percentages on the individual choices later on:

```
$query = "SELECT count(*) AS num_total_votes
          FROM vote V
```

```
        WHERE V.ID = $poll";

$result = @mysql_query($query, $db) or die ("mysql error: " . mysql_error());
$row = mysql_fetch_array($result);
$num_total_votes = $row["num_total_votes"];
```

Now it's time for the big query that gets the counts for each vote. This is a perfect place to use the LEFT JOIN clause along with SQL grouping to classify all of the votes. Though this query is a little more complicated than anything we've shown in this book so far, it's easy to dissect and understand:

```
$query = "SELECT A.answer, A.answer_ID, count(V.answer_ID) as num_votes
            FROM answer A
        LEFT JOIN vote V
                ON V.ID = A.ID
                AND V.answer_ID = A.answer_ID
            WHERE A.ID = $poll
        GROUP BY A.answer_ID
        ORDER BY num_votes DESC, A.answer ASC
";

$result = @mysql_query($query, $db) or die ("mysql error: " . mysql_error());
```

With the query results ready to roll, we prepare the HTML header and the first piece of the page:

```
print "<html><head><title>Poll: $question</title></head><body>";
print '<ul style="list-style-type: none; font-size: 12px;">';
print '<li style="font-weight: bold; padding-bottom: 10px;">';
print "Poll #$poll: $question";
print '</li>';
```

Then we iterate through each choice and display the results for each choice:

```
while ($row = mysql_fetch_array($result)) {
    if ($num_total_votes != 0) {
        $pct = sprintf("%.2f", 100.0 * $row["num_votes"] / $num_total_votes);
    } else {
        $pct = "0";
    }
    $boxwidth = strval(1 + intval($pct)) . "px";
    print '<li style="clear: left;">';
    print "$row[answer]";
    print "</li>";
    print '<li style="clear: left; padding-bottom: 7px;">';
    print '<div style="width: ' . $boxwidth . '; height: 15px;' .
          '; background: black; margin-right: 5px; float: left;">' .
          "</div>$pct%";
    print '</li>';
}
```

Finally, we wrap up the HTML with the total number of votes and the closing tags:

```
print '<li style="clear: left;">';
print "Total Votes: $num_total_votes";
print '</li>';
print '</ul>';
print '</body></html>';
?>
```

Of course, there is always room for improvement.

Hacking the Script

There are a number of things you can do to adapt this system for your own needs. First, you need a graphical interface for poll administration. You should have the ability not only to create new polls but also to activate or disable polls.

You can make the poll embeddable. That is, instead of having the poll come up in its own page, you can transform the poll into a set of functions. Then, when displaying a page, you can put the ballot in place with a <div> tag. The best part of an embedded poll is that you can make the results AJAX enabled. When the user clicks the Vote button, have the browser run JavaScript code that casts the vote and then replaces the ballot with the poll results.

Finally, you could think about other ways to ensure that users do not vote twice. To do so, you need to couple the vote table with a login system. Add an indexed field for a login ID, and then check this table instead of using a cookie to see if the user has already voted.

#75: Electronic Greeting Cards

Electronic greeting cards have been around almost since the Web became popular. They're nothing fancy. Just come up with some card content, add some code to display the content, then add a few features, such as notification of pickup, and you've got an e-card service.

The system in this section consists of four scripts. As with the preceding section, they contain a minimum amount of code; you can customize them as you see fit.

card_choose.php	Displays available cards
card_send.php	Presents a form for sending a particular card and sends the card
card_show.php	Displays the card to the recipient and notifies the sender that it has been viewed
card_include.php	Sets up the database connection and includes a utility function

The system requires two database tables. The first is named card_list and has this structure:

```
CREATE TABLE `card_list` (
`ID` INT NOT NULL AUTO_INCREMENT ,
`description` MEDIUMTEXT NOT NULL ,
`content` VARCHAR( 500 ) NOT NULL ,
`category` VARCHAR(20) NOT NULL ,
`width` INT NOT NULL ,
`height` INT NOT NULL ,
`thumbnail` VARCHAR(120),
PRIMARY KEY (`ID`)
) TYPE = MYISAM ;
```

Each row is a card. Set the content field to the HTML of the card that you want to show—it can be an image tag, an embedded Flash file, or even plaintext. The thumbnail field is for a preview on the card choice page; it's not required. Here is a simple example card:

```
INSERT INTO card_list
    (description, content, category, width, height, thumbnail)
    VALUES
    ("birthday card 1", "<b>Happy Birthday!</b> (1)", "birthday",
     600, 300, NULL );
```

The cards_sent table tracks sent cards. When you first implement the system, this table is empty:

```
CREATE TABLE `cards_sent` (
`sent_ID` INT NOT NULL AUTO_INCREMENT ,
`sender_email` VARCHAR( 50 ) NOT NULL ,
`sender_name` VARCHAR( 50 ) NOT NULL ,
`recip_email` VARCHAR( 50 ) NOT NULL ,
`recip_name` VARCHAR( 50 ) NOT NULL ,
`message` MEDIUMTEXT NOT NULL ,
`token` VARCHAR (32) NOT NULL ,
`ID` INT NOT NULL ,
`notified` TINYINT NULL ,
PRIMARY KEY ( `sent_ID` )
) TYPE = MYISAM ;
```

Here is card_include.php, the script that configures the MySQL connection and contains a function named card_display():

```php
<?php
$connection = @mysql_connect("localhost","db_login","db_password") or die(mysql_error());
$db = @mysql_select_db("wcphp", $connection) or die(mysql_error());

function display_card($card) {
    print '<div style="height: ' . $card["height"] . ';' .
                ' width: ' . $card["width"] . ';' .
```

```
            ' border: 1px solid; ' .
            ' text-align: center;">';
    print $card["content"];
    print '</div>';
}
?>
```

The $card parameter is an array with keys that reflects the field
names in the card_list table. Therefore, you can pass a row obtained from
mysql_fetch_array() directly to display_card().

Choosing a Card

The first stage of sending an electronic card is choosing a card, so let's look
at card_choose.php. This is nothing more than a loop that displays a menu
of the available cards, so we'll start it with some HTML to configure the
header and a few CSS classes:

```
<html><head>
<title>Choose a Card - e-cards</title>
<style>
table.choose { font-family: sans-serif; font-size: 12px; }
table.choose th { text-align: left; }
</style>
</head>
<body>
```

Starting with the actual PHP, we load the database configuration and
then look for the available cards with a query:

```
<?php
require_once("card_include.php");

/* Look up the cards. */
$sql = "SELECT ID, thumbnail, description, category
          FROM card_list
        ORDER BY category, description";

$result = @mysql_query($sql, $connection) or die (mysql_error());
```

If there are no cards, we indicate this problem. Otherwise, we indicate
how many cards are available and start HTML table formatting for the cards.
Each card will have its own row in the HTML table.

```
if (mysql_num_rows($result) == 0) {
    die('No cards listed.');
}
$num_cards = mysql_num_rows($result);
$plural = ($num_cards == 1) ? "card" : "cards";
```

```
print "$num_cards $plural available:<br />";
print "(click card to send)<br />";
print '<table class="choose">';
print "<tr><th>Category</th><th>Name</th><th>Thumbnail</th></tr>";
```

We're ready to print all of the table rows for the cards. This is a relatively straightforward loop and does not require formatting intervention because we specified it in the HTML header. Notice that there is a reference to the next script, card_send.php.

```
while($row = mysql_fetch_array($result)) {
    $link = "card_send.php?ID=$row[ID]";
    print '<tr>';
    print "<td>$row[category]</td>";
    print "<td><a href=\"$link\">$row[description]</a></td>";
    if ($row["thumbnail"]) {
        print "<td><a href=\"$link\">
                    <img src=\"$row[thumbnail]\" /></a></td>";
    } else {
        print "<td>(no thumbnail)</td>";
    }
    print "</tr>";
}
```

We wrap it up with the closing tags. Technically, the </table> tag could go into the literal HTML section, but because the opening tag came from a print statement, it doesn't hurt to be consistent, because we may eventually copy this code to another script.

```
print "</table>";
?>
</body>
</html>
```

When the script runs, it looks like Figure 12-3.

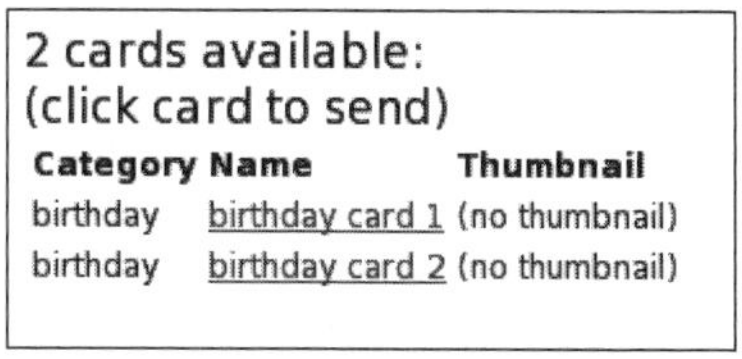

Sending the Card

After choosing a card, the user fills out a form with the recipient, sender, and message and sends the card notification on its way.

2 cards available: (click card to send)		
Category	**Name**	**Thumbnail**
birthday	birthday card 1	(no thumbnail)
birthday	birthday card 2	(no thumbnail)

Figure 12-3: Card choice menu

As with many scripts of this type, card_send.php handles both functions, so it's important to watch the control flow. When presenting the form, the script takes a card ID parameter named ID. When it accepts the form, there are several additional parameters: sender_email, sender_name, recip_email, recip_name, and message.

The script starts by validating the card ID and looking up the card in the database:

```php
<?php
require_once("card_include.php");

/* Validate card ID. */
$ID = $_REQUEST['ID'];
if ((!is_numeric($ID)) || ($ID == '') || ($ID < 1) ) {
    die("Invalid ID");
}

$sql = "SELECT ID, category, content, width, height, description
        FROM card_list
      WHERE ID = $ID";

$result = @mysql_query($sql, $connection) or die (mysql_error());
if (mysql_num_rows($result) == 0) {
    die('Invalid ID.');
}
$card = mysql_fetch_array($result);
```

Now it's time to see whether we're showing the form or sending the card by checking a parameter. We'll start with the case where we're sending the card. The first order of business is to check out the input parameters. The methods we'll use are perfunctory; it's likely that you'll want to add either a CAPTCHA (see "#66: Creating a CAPTCHA (Security) Image" on page 129) or some sort of check for a valid email address format.

```php
/* Determine mode - Are we displaying or sending a card? */
if (isset($_POST['recip_email'])) {
    /* Sending card */

    /* Check and clean data. */
    $send_email = substr($_POST['sender_email'], 0, 50);
    $send_name = substr($_POST['sender_name'], 0, 50);
    $rec_email = substr($_POST['recip_email'], 0, 50);
    $rec_name = substr($_POST['recip_name'], 0, 50);
    $message = substr($_POST['message'], 0, 600);
    $message = strip_tags($message);
    $rec_name = strip_tags($rec_name);
    $send_name = strip_tags($send_name);

    if ($_POST['message'] == '') {
        die("You must give a message!");
    }
```

The script just stripped any HTML tags from the message, but you probably want to put some sort of formatting in there, so we'll use the autop() function from "#42: Converting Plaintext into HTML-Ready Markup" on page 77.

```
/* Transform the text message into HTML. */
require("autop.php");
$message = autop($message);
```

Now it's time to create a means for the recipient to see the personalized message through a unique token. Although it's not technically unique, the chance of an MD5 hash repeating over the following domain is nearly zero, so we use it for simplicity:

```
/* Create a pickup token. */
$token = md5(strval(time()) . $send_email . $rec_email . $ID);
```

The reason we don't use a numeric auto-incrementing identifier for the pickup token is that it's too easy to guess. That said, it's time to insert the card information into the cards_sent table:

```
/* Insert the row into sent cards. */
$sql = 'INSERT INTO cards_sent
                    (sender_email, sender_name, message,
                     recip_email, recip_name, token, ID)
                VALUES
      ("' . $send_email . '", "' .
      mysql_escape_string($send_name) . '", "' .
      mysql_escape_string($message) . '", "' .
      $rec_email . '", "' .
      mysql_escape_string($rec_name) . '", "' .
      $token . '", ' .
      $ID . ')';
$result = @mysql_query($sql, $connection) or die (mysql_error());
```

Use PHPMailer (from "#64: Using PHPMailer to Send Mail" on page 120) to send the pickup message to the recipient:

```
/* PHPMailer class for sending mail */
    include_once("phpmailer/class.phpmailer.php");
    $mail = new PHPMailer;

    $mail->ClearAddresses();
    $mail->AddAddress($rec_email, $rec_name);
    print "$rec_email, $rec_name<br />";
    $mail->From = 'cards@example.com';
    $mail->FromName = $send_name;
    $mail->Subject = "You have received an e-card from $send_name!";
    $mail->Body = "You have received an e-card!\n";
    $mail->Body .= "Please go to
    http://www.example.com/card_show.php?token=$token to view it.\n\n";
    $mail->Body .= "Sincerely,\nThose e-card guys";

    if ($mail->Send()) {
```

```
      print 'Your e-card was sent!';
   } else {
      print 'There was an error: ' . $mail->ErrorInfo;
   }
```

That's all there is to sending the card when given form data. Notice the reference in the outgoing email message to the final script, card_show.php, and its token parameter. You will need to modify parts of the preceding fragment, specifically the URL, which you may want to place in card_include .php. In addition, this script should redirect the user to another page that looks better.

If we're just showing the form, the task boils down to busy work:

```
} else {
   /* Display card and sending form. */

   print '<span style="font-family: sans-serif; font-size: 12px;">';
   print '<form action="card_send.php" method="post">';

   print '<input name="ID" type="hidden" value="' . $card['ID'] . '">';
   display_card($card);
   print '<br />';

   ?>
   Recipient Email:<br />
   <input name="recip_email" type="text" size="30" maxlength="50">
   <br /><br />
   Recipient Name:<br />
   <input name="recip_name" type="text" size="30" maxlength="50">
   <br /><br />
   Message (No HTML, 600 characters max):<br />
   <textarea name="message" cols="40" rows="6"></textarea>
   <br /><br />
   Sender Email:<br />
   <input name="sender_email" type="text" size="30" maxlength="50">
   <br /><br />
   Sender Name:<br />
   <input name="sender_name" type="text" size="30" maxlength="50"></td></tr>
   <br /><br />
   <input name="" type="submit" value="Send Your Card!"></td></tr>
   </form>
   </span>
   <?php
}
?>
```

Figure 12-4 shows the form.

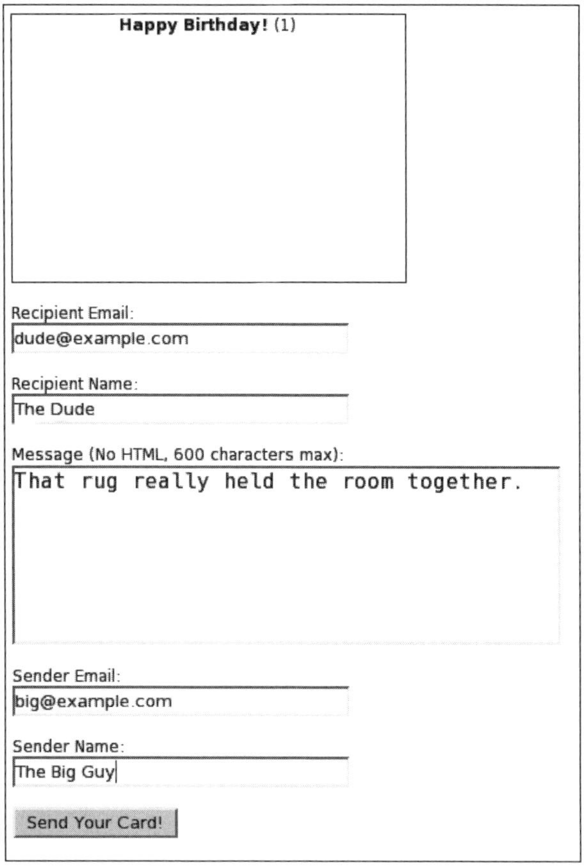

```
Happy Birthday! (1)




Recipient Email:
dude@example.com

Recipient Name:
The Dude

Message (No HTML, 600 characters max):
That  rug  really  held  the  room  together.




Sender Email:
big@example.com

Sender Name:
The Big Guy

[Send Your Card!]
```

Figure 12-4: Sending a card

Viewing the Card

We're almost finished; all we need now is the card_show.php script that shows the card to the recipient and notifies the sender that the card was picked up. The first part is like nearly any other script; it loads the include files and sanitizes the input parameters. In this case, we throw out any nonalphanumeric characters in the token parameter:

```php
<?php
require_once("card_include.php");
$token = preg_replace('/[^a-z0-9]/', '', $_REQUEST['token']);
```

We need to know the card content and the details of this particular message. That's easy to do by joining the card_list and cards_sent tables on the ID fields and looking up by the token.

```
$sql = "SELECT S.sender_name, S.sender_email, S.message,
                S.recip_name, S.recip_email, S.notified,
                C.content, C.width, C.height
            FROM cards_sent S, card_list C
          WHERE C.ID = S.ID
            AND S.token = '$token'";

$result = @mysql_query($sql, $connection) or die (mysql_error());
if (mysql_num_rows($result) == 0) {
    die('Invalid card.');
}

$row = mysql_fetch_array($result);
```

Notice the notified field in cards_sent; this indicates whether or not the card has already been viewed. It should always be set to 0 just after sending the card.

Printing the card and message is dull work, but thankfully we have that display_card() function from card_include.php, so we don't have to remember how to display based on the database fields.

```
print '<span style="font-family: sans-serif; font-size: 12px">';
print '<p>A card for you!</p>';

display_card($row);
print '<br />';

print '<strong>' . stripslashes($row["sender_name"]) . '</strong> writes:';
print '<br />';
print stripslashes($row["message"]);
```

Now let's get around to notification. Obviously, we don't want to send another email message to the sender if this is not the first time the card has been viewed, so we check for that first. As we did in card_send.php, we'll use PHPMailer to send the email message:

```
if (!$row['notified']) {
    /* Notify sender that the message was picked up. */
    include_once("phpmailer/class.phpmailer.php");
    $mail = new PHPMailer;
    $mail->ClearAddresses();
    $mail->AddAddress($row['sender_email'], $row['sender_name']);
    $mail->From = 'example@example.com';
    $mail->FromName = 'E-card People';
    $mail->Subject = 'e-card retrieved';
    $mail->Body = "Your e-card to $row[recip_name] has been picked up.

        Sincerely,
        Those e-card guys";
    $mail->Send();
```

And now we update the `notified` field for the card in the cards_sent table so that this is the only notification message that will go out:

```
$sql = "UPDATE cards_sent
            SET notified = 1
            WHERE token = '$token'";
@mysql_query($sql, $connection);
}
?>
```

Figure 12-5 shows what the recipient sees from card_show.php. Obviously, this is not terribly fancy, but you, as a master of HTML, will have no trouble jazzing it up, right?

Hacking the Script

There are a number of ways to improve this system. One of the first and most important improvements is to install a CAPTCHA or similar system so that it's hard to automate sending the cards as spam (see "#66: Creating a CAPTCHA (Security) Image" on page 129).

A card for you!

Happy Birthday! (1)

The Big Guy writes:

That rug really held the room together.

Figure 12-5: The card, as viewed by the recipient

Another important piece would be an administration tool to let you add, edit, and disable cards. When you get to a certain number of cards, it becomes difficult to display and manage them on a single page, so you should add a search function.

#76: A Blogging System

Blogs are common because they're very easy to write—all you really need is a system to keep track of dates and content. The basic blog that appears here includes tools for adding entries, adding comments, and viewing entries. The system stores entries and comments in a MySQL database and uses Smarty for display templates.

Here is the main table for blog entries, originally named blog_entries:

```
CREATE TABLE `blog_entries` (
`ID` INT NOT NULL AUTO_INCREMENT ,
`title` VARCHAR( 120 ) NOT NULL ,
`content` TEXT NOT NULL ,
`teaser` TINYTEXT NOT NULL ,
`entry_time` DATETIME NOT NULL ,
```

```
`category` VARCHAR( 12 ) NOT NULL ,
PRIMARY KEY ( `ID` )
) TYPE = MYISAM ;
```

Most of these fields are self explanatory. teaser is a snippet of the entry that contains no markup. Here is the blog_comments table:

```
CREATE TABLE `blog_comments` (
`comment_ID` INT AUTO_INCREMENT ,
`name` VARCHAR( 50 ) NOT NULL ,
`comment` TEXT NOT NULL ,
`comment_time` timestamp,
`ID` INT NOT NULL ,
PRIMARY KEY ( `comment_ID` )
) TYPE = MYISAM ;
```

The reason the comment_time field has a timestamp type is that we don't intend to make comments editable; once a comment is up, it's not going to change, so there is no need to manually set the date.

As with our other scripts, a configuration file called blog_config.php configures the MySQL connection and creates a Smarty object. With this default configuration, the Smarty templates will go in the templates directory:

```
<?php
session_start();
$connection = @mysql_connect("localhost","login","password") or die("Couldn't connect.");
$db = @mysql_select_db("wcphp", $connection) or die(mysql_error());
require_once ("smarty/Smarty.class.php");
$smarty = new Smarty();
?>
```

Here is an overview of the four scripts in the system:

blog_edit.php	Edits and adds new blog entries
blog_index.php	Shows a listing of blog entries
blog_display.php	Displays an individual blog entry
blog_comment.php	Adds a comment to a blog entry

Creating Blog Entries

It's important to be able to add content before doing anything else. Therefore, let's go straight to the entry editor. With this script, we'll really start to see how much cleaner it is to use Smarty to separate the HTML templates from PHP. Let's start with the template called templates/blog_edit.tpl:

```
<html><head>
<title>{$title}</title>
{literal}
<style>
h1 {
```

```
        font-family: sans-serif;
        font-size: 20px;
}
table.inputfields {
        font-family: sans-serif;
        font-size: 12px;
}
table.inputfields td {
        vertical-align: top;
}
</style>
{/literal}
</head>
<body>
<h1>New Blog Entry</h1>
<form method="post" action="blog_edit.php">
<table class="inputfields">
<tr> <td>Title:</td><td><input name="title" type="text" /></td> </tr>
<tr> <td>Body:</td>
     <td><textarea name="content" rows="15" cols="40"></textarea></td>
</tr>
<tr> <td>Category:</td><td><input name="category" type="text" /> </tr>
<tr> <td /><td><input name="submit" type="submit" value="Post" /></td> </tr>
</table>
</form>
</body>
</html>
```

This template is nothing more than a form with title, content, and category fields, sent via the POST method to blog_edit.php. Figure 12-6 shows how a browser renders this form when it is sent through Smarty.

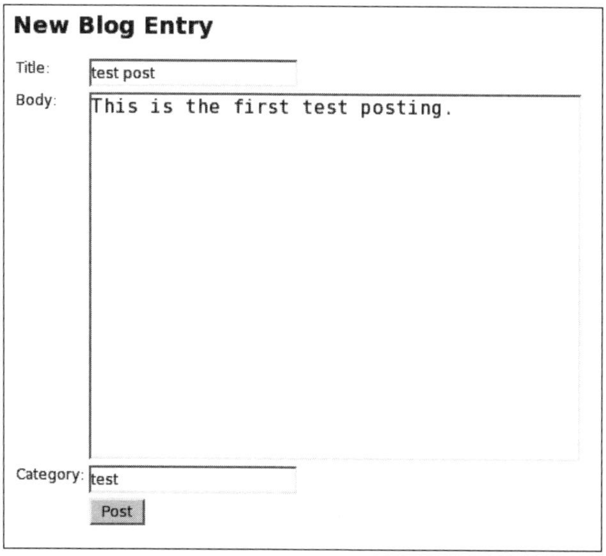

Figure 12-6: Posting a blog entry

And here is blog_edit.php, a two-mode script. If it is taking input from the preceding form, it sanitizes the input fields, inserts the new entry into the database, and then redirects the user to display the new entry:

```php
<?php
require_once("blog_config.php");

if ($_REQUEST["submit"]) {
    $content = mysql_escape_string(strip_tags($_REQUEST["content"],
                                   "<a><i><b><img>"));
    $teaser = substr(strip_tags($content), 0, 80);
    $title = mysql_escape_string(strip_tags($_REQUEST["title"]));
    $category = mysql_escape_string(strip_tags($_REQUEST["category"]));
    $q = "INSERT INTO blog_entries
               (title, content, category, teaser, entry_time)
        VALUES ('$title', '$content', '$category', '$teaser', now())";
    mysql_query($q, $connection) or die(mysql_error());
    $id = mysql_insert_id($connection);
    header("Location: blog_display.php?ID=$id");
```

Notice the use of mysql_insert_id(). This handy function returns the value of the last inserted AUTO_INCREMENT database field. In this case, it was the ID field of the new blog_entries row, so we can use it to send the user to the display page for the new entry.

If we're just displaying the blog entry form rather than inserting an entry, all we need to do is ask Smarty to display it:

```php
} else {
    $smarty->assign("title", "blog: post an entry");
    $smarty->display("blog_edit.tpl");
}
?>
```

Technically, you could hardcode the title into the template, but assigning one variable gets you ready for making a fancier editor if you need one.

Displaying an Entry

The blog_display.php script must output three items: a blog entry, the comments to the blog, and a form that allows users to add their own comments. Let's first examine these three components in templates/blog_display.tpl. The first part is header information and a piece of JavaScript that we'll use later on to show the comment form:

```html
<html><head>
<title>{$title}</title>
{literal}
<style>
h1 {
    font-family: sans-serif;
    font-size: 20px;
```

```
}
h4 {
    font-family: sans-serif;
    font-size: 12px;
}
.content {
    font-family: sans-serif;
    font-size: 12px;
}
</style>
<script>
function show_cform() {
    o = document.getElementById("comment_form");
    if (o) { o.style.display = ""; }
    o = document.getElementById("comment_link");
    if (o) { o.style.display = "none"; }
}
</script>
{/literal}
</head>
```

Now comes the section for the blog entry content. This is relatively simple, because the structure is static. Notice the blog_index.php link, which will be our last script:

```
<body>
<span class="content">
<a href="blog_index.php">my blog</a>
<h1>{$title}</h1>
{$date}
<p>
{$content}
</p>
Category: {$category}<br />
<br />
```

For the blog comments, Smarty's {section} feature allows us to show an arbitrary number of comments by iterating through them in an array. In this case, we'll assign the $comments variable to an array of comments. Each comment is itself an array, with name, time, and comment keys for access to the individual comment content. Smarty iterates through the comments, displaying the contents of this section for each one, allowing for a very compact representation. If you're lost, skip ahead to see how blog_display.php assigns the $comments variable.

```
<h4>Comments</h4>
{section name=i loop=$comments}
  <b>{$comments[i].name}</b> ({$comments[i].time})<br />
  {$comments[i].comment}
  <br /><br />
{/section}
```

Finally, we need to display the form for allowing the user to add a comment. For this, we'll use a little trick; instead of showing the form outright, we'll keep it hidden until the user clicks the JavaScript link labeled *Add a Comment*. The action for the form is blog_comment.php.

```
<div id="comment_link">
  <a href="javascript:show_cform();">Add a Comment</a>
</div>
<div id="comment_form" style="display: none;">
<form method="post" action="blog_comment.php">
<input type="hidden" name="ID" value="{$id}">
Your name:<br />
<input name="name" type="text" />
<br /><br />
Comment:<br />
<textarea name="comment" rows="8" cols="40"></textarea>
<br />
<input type="submit" value="Post comment">
</form>
</div>
</span>
</body>
</html>
```

Figure 12-7 shows an example entry display with a hidden comment form.

Figure 12-7: Blog entry (with comments)

With all of the messy HTML behind us, blog_display.php comes together very quickly. We follow the usual initial screenplay of verifying the ID input parameter and looking up the entry in the database:

```
<?php
require_once("blog_config.php");
$ID = intval($_REQUEST['ID']);

$query = "SELECT title, category, content,
                UNIX_TIMESTAMP(entry_time) AS entry_time
            FROM blog_entries
```

```
              WHERE ID = $ID";

$result = @mysql_query($query, $connection) or die(mysql_error());

if (mysql_num_rows($result) == 0) {
    die('Invalid ID.');
}
```

If we get this far, the entry is valid, so let's assign its data to the Smarty object:

```
$row = mysql_fetch_array($result);
$smarty->assign("title", $row["title"]);
$smarty->assign("content", $row["content"]);
$smarty->assign("category", $row["category"]);
$smarty->assign("date", date("F dS Y, h:ia", $row["entry_time"]));
$smarty->assign("id", $ID);
```

Now we look up the comments with a very simple MySQL query (there is no need to join tables):

```
/* Look up comments. */
$query = "SELECT comment, name,
                 UNIX_TIMESTAMP(comment_time) AS comment_time
            FROM blog_comments
           WHERE ID = $ID
        ORDER BY comment_time ASC";

$result = @mysql_query($query, $connection) or die (mysql_error());
```

It's time to do the dirty work of placing the comments into an array of arrays called $comments and assigning that to the Smarty $comments variable. Typically, this kind of code is a mess of print statements for tag closings and openings, but as previously mentioned, with Smarty's {section} feature, it's a piece of cake:

```
$comments = array();
while ($row = mysql_fetch_array($result)) {
    $comments[] = array(
        "name"    => $row["name"],
        "comment" => $row["comment"],
        "time"    => date("F dS Y, h:ia", $row["comment_time"]),
    );
}
$smarty->assign("comments", $comments);
```

There's nothing left to do now but process the template.

```
/* Display page. */
$smarty->display("blog_display.tpl");
?>
```

Now, what do we do when a user adds a comment?

Adding Comments

The script that adds comments to entries, blog_comment.php, is the only one in this system that doesn't have a template, because it doesn't display anything. Recall from the preceding section that it takes three parameters: ID, comment, and name, for the entry ID, comment content, and name of the person making the comment. The first step is to make sure that entry ID is valid:

```php
<?php
require_once("blog_config.php");

$ID = intval($_REQUEST["ID"]);
/* Look up the blog posting; make sure it's real. */
$query = "SELECT title FROM blog_entries WHERE ID = $ID";
$result = mysql_query($query, $connection) or die(mysql_error());
if (mysql_num_rows($result) != 1) {
    header("Location: blog_index.php");
    exit;
}
```

Then we sanitize the comments and name by removing all HTML inside. If there's still something left by the time we're through with that, we insert it into blog_comments table:

```php
$name = mysql_escape_string(strip_tags($_REQUEST["name"]));
$comment = mysql_escape_string(strip_tags($_REQUEST["comment"]));
$comment = nl2br($comment);

if (!empty($name) && !empty($comment)) {
    $query = "INSERT INTO blog_comments
                (ID, comment, name)
            VALUES ($ID, '$comment', '$name')";
    mysql_query($query, $connection) or die(mysql_error());
}
```

When this is complete, we finish by sending the user back to the blog entry page, which now (in theory) includes the user's own two cents:

```php
header("Location: blog_display.php?ID=$ID");
?>
```

The only thing we're missing in our blog system now is an index page.

Creating a Blog Index

The greeting page that shows the most recent blog entries is similar to the blog entry page, because it uses the Smarty {section} feature to cut down on iteration clutter.

Let's look at the templates/blog_index.tpl file, which starts with this standard header information:

```
<html><head>
<title>{$title}</title>
{literal}
<style>
table.entries {
    font-size: 12px;
}
table.entries td {
    padding-bottom: 7px;
}
.headline {
    font-size: 14px;
    font-weight: bold;
}
</style>
{/literal}
</head>
<body>
<a href="blog_index.php">my blog</a>
```

The blog index will be able to display entries by category if necessary. The next part shows the current category if there is one:

```
{if $category}
    <br />
    Category: {$category}
{/if}
```

Now we use {section} to iterate over the $blog_items variable, which is an array of arrays, each one containing information about a blog entry:

```
<br />
<table class="entries">
{section name=i loop=$blog_items}
<tr><td>
  <span class="headline">
  <a href="blog_display.php?ID={$blog_items[i].ID}">{$blog_items[i].title}</a>
  </span>
  <br />
  {$blog_items[i].date}<br />
  {$blog_items[i].teaser}<br />
  Category: <a href="blog_index.php?category={$blog_items[i].category_parm}">
          {$blog_items[i].category}
        </a>
</td></tr>
{/section}
</table>
</body>
</html>
```

The blog_index.php script starts off by checking for a category parameter. If this parameter exists, the index should display only entries of that category. To do so, create an SQL WHERE clause to limit the query that you will see very soon, but make sure that you sanitize the input parameter first. If there is no category, set its variables to empty strings.

```php
<?php
require_once("blog_config.php");

if ($_REQUEST["category"]) {
    $category = mysql_escape_string($_REQUEST["category"]);
    $where_clause = "WHERE category = '$category'";
    $smarty->assign("category", $category);
} else {
    $where_clause = "";
    $smarty->assign("category", "");
}
```

Formulate and run the SQL query as follows:

```php
$sql = "SELECT title, category, teaser,
            UNIX_TIMESTAMP(entry_time) AS entry_time, ID
        FROM blog_entries
            $where_clause
    ORDER BY entry_time DESC
        LIMIT 0, 20";
$result = @mysql_query($sql, $connection) or die (mysql_error());
if (mysql_num_rows($result) == 0) {
        die('No entries in this blog.');
}
```

Assuming that the query was successful, you can go straight to building the array that you're going to assign to the $blog_items Smarty variable:

```php
$items = array();
while ($row = mysql_fetch_array($result)) {
    $items[] = array(
        "ID"           => $row["ID"],
        "date"         => date("F dS Y, h:ia", $row['entry_time']),
        "title"        => $row["title"],
        "teaser"       => $row["teaser"],
        "category"     => $row["category"],
        "category_parm" => urlencode($row["category"]),
    );
}
$smarty->assign("blog_items", $items);
```

Finish by assigning the title and displaying the template (see Figure 12-8 for the final result):

```
$smarty->assign("title", "blog: index");
$smarty->display("blog_index.tpl");
?>
```

Figure 12-8: Blog entry index

Hacking the Script

Blogs were made for hacking. There are many features that you can add to this system, and all of them build upon or expand your PHP knowledge. Here are a few sample ideas:

Archive   Once you start to have more than a few entries, you need to split up the index by pages. "#3: Creating Previous/Next Links" on page 7 can help you with that.

RSS feed   Apply your knowledge of how to create web services from "#73: Building a Web Service" on page 151 to this system, and you've syndicated the blog.

Login and administration   As it stands, anyone can add entries to a blog. You can prevent that by requiring a login to add entries. Furthermore, you can add multiple blogs by adding usernames to the blog tables.

CAPTCHA for comments   If you have a blog, you're going to have spam comments. Eliminate them with the script that you saw in "#66: Creating a CAPTCHA (Security) Image" on page 129 or with Akismet.

Whatever you do, have fun with it!

APPENDIX

Several scripts in this book refer to a product_info table containing details of the inventory for a hypothetical store. Here is the table definition:

```sql
CREATE TABLE `product_info` (
  `product_name` varchar(50) default NULL,
  `product_id` int(10) default NULL,
  `category` enum('shoes','gloves','hats') default NULL,
  `price` double default NULL,
  PRIMARY KEY (`product_id`)
);
```

Once you have the table in place, you will probably want to provide some sample data:

```sql
INSERT INTO `product_info` VALUES ('Cowboy Boots',12,'shoes',19.99);
INSERT INTO `product_info` VALUES ('Slippers',17,'shoes',9.99);
INSERT INTO `product_info` VALUES ('Snowboarding Boots',15,'shoes',89.99);
INSERT INTO `product_info` VALUES ('Flip-Flops',19,'shoes',2.99);
INSERT INTO `product_info` VALUES ('Baseball',20,'hats',12.79);
```

Note that although the number in the product_id field is somewhat arbitrary, it must be unique for each row.

INDEX

dates, *continued*
    Unix time, 81–82
    verifying with checkdate(), 85
    verifying with strtotime(), 84
    working with, 81–90
DATETIME field type, 90
deleting files, 96
deleting substrings, 64
$dest_image, 138
dictionaries, pspell, 65–69
directories
    access to, 26–27
    permissions, 92–93
    uploading images to, 96–101
display() method, 15
display_errors setting, 24
dollar sign ($), 15–16, 70
DOM system, 145, 151
domains, 106
dot character. *See* period (.)
double quotes (")
    escaping, 26
    finding, 46
    Magic Quotes, 26
    strings and, 70

E

Eastern Standard Time, 83
e-card service, 162–171
electronic greeting cards, 162–171
email, 119–127
    attachments, 122–123
    authentication, 121
    greeting cards, 165–171
    HTML, 122
    junk, 120, 124
    passwords, 121
    PHPMailer, 120–123, 167
    sending, 119–127
    sendmail, 120–121, 123
    SMTP, 120, 121, 123
    spam, 120, 124
    validating addresses, 56–57,
        124, 166
    verifying user accounts with,
        124–127
--enable-soap parameter, 149

encryption
    arrays, 12
    vs. hashing, 40
    Mcrypt, 27, 41–43
    passwords, 117
    SSL, 111
epoch date, 81
equal sign (=), 20, 64
ereg() function, 69
error_log parameter, 24
error_reporting parameter, 24, 35
errors. *See also* troubleshooting
    arrays, 23
    during build process, 32
    common, 23–24
    file open, 96
    indexes, 23
    logging, 35
    permissions, 95
    printing, 155
    quotes and, 23
    reporting, 22–24, 35
    suppressing, 24
    variables, 23
escape sequences, 87
Excel (XLS) format, 101–102
Excel spreadsheets, 101–102
exec() function, 27, 35
execute permission, 92
expose_php parameter, 35
expressions, regular. *See* regular
        expressions
eXtensible Markup Language. *See*
        XML (eXtensible Markup
        Language)
extensions. *See also* libraries
    adding to PHP, 27–32
    checking for, 28–29
    examples of, 27–28
    finding, 28
    .gif, 136
    .gz, 30
    installing libraries, 30–32
    .jpg, 122, 136
    .png, 136

F

fclose() function, 94
feof() function, 94

newlines, 77–78, 96
Next links, 7–11
nl2br( ) function, 77–78
null values, 46

O

OCR software, 133
online blogging systems, 171–181
online credit card transactions, 52–55
online greeting cards, 162–171
online polls, 156–162
open_basedir parameter, 35
open_basedir setting, 26–27
OpenSSL library, 142
Opera browser, 112–114
owner permission, 91

P

<p> tag, 79
$page_count( ) variable, 9
pages. *See* web pages
parentheses [( )], 71
parsers, 79, 142, 144–146, 150
passphrase, 41–43, 130–136
passthru( ) function, 35
passwords. *See also* authentication
    email, 121
    encrypted, 117
    database, 40–41
    generating, 43–44, 118
    guidelines, 41
    hashed, 40–41, 118
    login systems, 116–118
    MySQL, 2–4
    one-way security, 40–41
    passphrase, 41–43, 130–136
    random, 43–44
    storage of, 2–4
paths
    cookies, 106
    files, 94, 122
    to script, 3
patterns, repeating, 71
payment gateway, 52
PDF format, 28
period (.), 70, 71
Perl-compatible functions, 69–70

permissions
    directories, 92–93
    errors, 95
    execute, 92
    file, 91–93
    file deletion, 97
    group, 91
    owner, 91
    read, 92
    setting, 92–93
    world, 91
    write, 92
phone number validation, 57
<?php marker, 2
PHP
    adding extensions to, 27–32
    basics, 1–17
    case sensitivity of, 62–63
    configuring. *See* configuring PHP
    defaults, 20
    security, 33–44
    settings, 20–22
    SOAP and, 149–151
    version number, 35
PHP scripts. *See* scripts
phpinfo( ) function, 20, 21, 31, 130
phpinfo( ) script, 31
php.ini command, 20, 28
php.ini file, 20, 24, 26–27
PHPMailer, 120–123, 167
pipe symbol (|), 70, 71
plus sign (+), 71
.png extension, 136
PNG
    files, 136, 139
    format, 139
poll ID, 157–160
polls, online, 156–162
polygons, 132–133
popen function, 35
POSIX Extended functions, 69
$_POST array, 47, 49–52
POST parameter
    accessing pages, 143
    REST service, 142
    security risks, 25–26
predefined server variables, 47
preg_match( ) function, 70, 73

 # Electronic Frontier Foundation
Defending Freedom in the Digital World

Free Speech. Privacy. Innovation. Fair Use. Reverse Engineering. If you care about these rights in the digital world, then you should join the Electronic Frontier Foundation (EFF). EFF was founded in 1990 to protect the rights of users and developers of technology. EFF is the first to identify threats to basic rights online and to advocate on behalf of free expression in the digital age.

The Electronic Frontier Foundation Defends Your Rights!
Become a Member Today!
http://www.eff.org/support/

Current EFF projects include:

Protecting your fundamental right to vote. Widely publicized security flaws in computerized voting machines show that, though filled with potential, this technology is far from perfect. EFF is defending the open discussion of e-voting problems and is coordinating a national litigation strategy addressing issues arising from use of poorly developed and tested computerized voting machines.

Ensuring that you are not traceable through your things. Libraries, schools, the government and private sector businesses are adopting radio frequency identification tags, or RFIDs – a technology capable of pinpointing the physical location of whatever item the tags are embedded in. While this may seem like a convenient way to track items, it's also a convenient way to do something less benign: track people and their activities through their belongings. EFF is working to ensure that embrace of this technology does not erode your right to privacy.

Stopping the FBI from creating surveillance backdoors on the Internet. EFF is part of a coalition opposing the FBI's expansion of the Communications Assistance for Law Enforcement Act (CALEA), which would require that the wiretap capabilities built into the phone system be extended to the Internet, forcing ISPs to build backdoors for law enforcement.

Providing you with a means by which you can contact key decision-makers on cyber-liberties issues. EFF maintains an action center that provides alerts on technology, civil liberties issues and pending legislation to more than 50,000 subscribers. EFF also generates a weekly online newsletter, EFFector, and a blog that provides up-to-the minute information and commentary.

Defending your right to listen to and copy digital music and movies. The entertainment industry has been overzealous in trying to protect its copyrights, often decimating fair use rights in the process. EFF is standing up to the movie and music industries on several fronts.

Check out all of the things we're working on at http://www.eff.org and join today or make a donation to support the fight to defend freedom online.

ELECTRONIC FRONTIER FOUNDATION · 454 SHOTWELL STREET · SAN FRANCISCO, CA 94110 · 415.436.9333

WEBBOTS, SPIDERS, AND SCREEN SCRAPERS
A Guide to Developing Internet Agents with PHP/CURL

by MICHAEL SCHRENK

The Internet is bigger and better than a mere browser allows. *Webbots, Spiders, and Screen Scrapers* is for programmers, webbies, and business managers looking to unlock the competitive advantages of the Internet in nontraditional ways. Learn how to write stealthy webbots that read email, emulate online forms, auto-authenticate, manage cookies, and handle encryption. Sample projects show how to create more sophisticated webbots and spiders to track online prices, create anonymous browsing environments, bid on auctions in their closing moments, and more.

APRIL 2007, 328 PP., $39.95 ($49.95 CDN)
ISBN 978-1-59327-120-6

OBJECT-ORIENTED PHP
Concepts, Technique, and Code

by PETER LAVIN

Object-Oriented PHP shows developers how to take advantage of the new object-oriented features of PHP. Working from concrete examples, the book begins with code compatible with PHP 4 and 5, and then focuses on object orientation in PHP 5. The author's practical approach uses numerous code examples, which will help developers get up to speed quickly and show them how to apply what they've learned to everyday situations. All code samples are available for download on the book's companion website.

JUNE 2006, 216 PP., $29.95 ($38.95 CDN)
ISBN 978-1-59327-077-3

THE BOOK OF JAVASCRIPT, 2ND EDITION
A Practical Guide to Interactive Web Pages

by THAU!

This book teaches readers how to add interactivity, animation, and other tricks to their websites with JavaScript. Rather than provide a series of cut-and-paste scripts, thau! takes the reader through real-world JavaScript code examples with an emphasis on understanding. Each chapter focuses on a few important JavaScript features, shows how professional websites incorporate them, and shows readers how they might add those features to their own websites. This thoroughly updated and completely reworked second edition includes coverage of Ajax, revised appendices, and new examples throughout.

DECEMBER 2006, 528 PP., $39.95 ($49.95 CDN)
ISBN 978-1-59327-106-0

WICKED COOL JAVA
Code Bits, Open-Source Libraries, and Project Ideas

by BRIAN D. EUBANKS

Wicked Cool Java contains 101 fun, interesting, and useful ways to get more out of Java. Full of example code and ideas for combining that code into useful projects, this book is perfect for hobbyists and professionals looking for tips and open source projects to enhance their code and make their jobs easier. Topics include converting a non-XML text structure into XML using a parser generator, experimenting with a Java simulator for the Cell Matrix, creating dynamic music and sound in Java, working with open source class libraries for scientific and mathematical applications, and much more.

NOVEMBER 2005, 248 PP., $29.95 ($40.95 CDN)
ISBN 978-1-59327-061-2

RUBY BY EXAMPLE
Concepts and Code

by KEVIN C. BAIRD

There may be no better way to learn how to program than by dissecting real, representative examples written in your language of choice. *Ruby by Example* analyzes a series of Ruby scripts, examining how the code works, explaining the concepts it illustrates, and showing how to modify it to suit your needs. Baird's examples demonstrate key features of the language (such as inheritance, encapsulation, higher-order functions, and recursion), while simultaneously solving difficult problems (such as validating XML, creating a bilingual program, and creating command-line interfaces). Each chapter builds upon the previous one, and each key concept is highlighted in the margin to make it easier for you to navigate through the book.

JUNE 2007, 312 PP., $29.95 ($37.95 CDN)
ISBN 978-1-59327-148-0

PHONE:
800.420.7240 OR
415.863.9900
MONDAY THROUGH FRIDAY,
9 A.M. TO 5 P.M. (PST)

FAX:
415.863.9950
24 HOURS A DAY,
7 DAYS A WEEK

EMAIL:
SALES@NOSTARCH.COM

WEB:
WWW.NOSTARCH.COM

MAIL:
NO STARCH PRESS
555 DE HARO ST, SUITE 250
SAN FRANCISCO, CA 94107
USA

UPDATES

Visit *http://www.nostarch.com/wcphp.htm* for updates, errata, and other information.

COLOPHON

The fonts used in *Wicked Cool PHP* are New Baskerville, Futura, and Dogma.

The book was printed and bound at Malloy Incorporated in Ann Arbor, Michigan. The paper is Glatfelter Spring Forge 60# Smooth Antique, which is certified by the Sustainable Forestry Initiative (SFI). The book uses a RepKover binding, which allows it to lay flat when open.